# Data Mesh Design

## A Practical Pipeline Design Guide for Analytics, Data Science and Machine Learning

**Bruno Freitag**

Technics Publications
SEDONA, ARIZONA

115 Linda Vista
Sedona, AZ 86336 USA

https://www.TechnicsPub.com

Edited by Sadie Hoberman

Cover design by Lorena Molinari

First Printing 2023

Copyright © 2023 by Bruno Freitag

| | |
|---|---|
| ISBN, print ed. | 9781634622158 |
| ISBN, Kindle ed. | 9781634622264 |
| ISBN, ePub ed. | 9781634622271 |
| ISBN, PDF ed. | 9781634622295 |

Library of Congress Control Number: 2023937746

# Acknowledgments

I want to thank the countless people that contributed directly or indirectly to this book, mostly by engaging in passionate discussions where we did not always agree. They ultimately sharpened the thinking and helped distill the essence. Many of them may not even be aware of the influence they have had. This acknowledgment list is by no means complete but starts with Dr. W. Hett who planted the seed for thinking in structured data many decades ago, and Fredy Wunderlich, who taught me data models. More recently, Abhishek Bhattacharya, Alex Meadows, Harish Krishnamoorthy, Ludovic Dumaine, Yannick Flores, and countless others have contributed to the solution thinking presented in this book.

Lastly, I want to thank Peter Mararo, Steve Hoberman, and others for their thorough editorial review. A big thanks go to the people at Syngenta, not the least Aart Labee, for supporting the book and Ryan Mastro, now at IBM consulting, who had faith in my concepts when they were still immature and supported materializing them. Without them, what would have remained great theory is practice now.

Thank you,

Bruno Freitag

PS: This book is the result of countless errors, short-sighted designs, and mistakes I have made during my career and a summary of what I should have done.

# Contents

# List of Figures

# Sample Code

# Introduction

There are countless books on data literacy, data science, machine learning, and other data-related topics. So why this book? Data democratization, machine learning, and in-memory data analysis tools raised expectations for data pipelines. Pipelines require real-time, integrated, and reusable data in ever-changing combinations. Traditional data warehouse designs and data vaults become complex very quickly if applied at the enterprise level. We can simplify them through modular design, delivering faster results and facilitating data mesh integration. This book describes an agile approach that scales linearly with growing needs and avoids inflationary complexity. It is a practical guide for integrated data marts in large-scale enterprises within complex environments. It satisfies three basic needs:

- Data scientists needing integrated data to train their models.
- Self-service and data visualization engineers needing flexible data exploration.
- Data federation for ownership and access.

The first two spawn into self-service and the third into a data mesh. Our approach meets these needs through a set of modular data marts and processes for using these marts. Both processes handle large integrated data volumes at once. The organization's need for an independent federated approach leads to the specific design of those modular data marts.

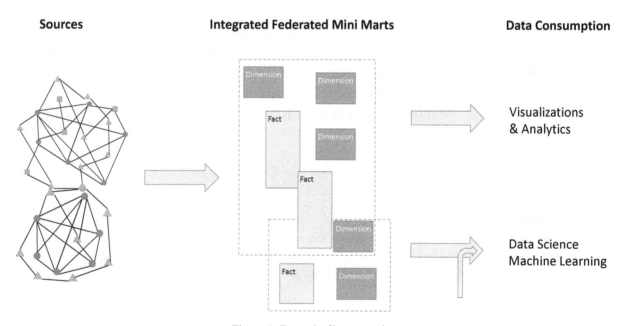

Figure 1: Data pipeline overview

This book is about techniques and methodology for modular data marts that can scale enterprise wide.

It is about data design, data engineering, and processes for a modular, agile, and cost-effective enterprise data pipeline, underpinning data science, machine learning, and data analysis in its many sizes, shapes, and forms. In addition, we look at using the data for various purposes, including for machine learning in combination with "one-off" data and we explore data catalog, lineage, and transition challenges.

To baseline our thoughts, let's briefly recap the history of databases and how they evolved from the Sumerian times to current technologies. Databases existed long before the computer age. Sumerian tablets, made of clay, were used to index medical prescriptions and determine taxes. Shipping manifests were used to list cargo. Card catalogs succeeded them while punch cards arrived much later with the advent of computers. Punch cards were, in essence, flat data files—a simple consecutive list of records. This was a slow way to search and maintain, especially with increasing volume. New approaches were needed. Hierarchical models emerged in the mid-'60s, including IBM's IMS system, which was a tree-like structure.

Ted Codd and later C.J. Date first proposed the relational data model in the '70s. This was a system of related tables with keys, matching data based on fields pointing between them. Their ideas sparked many implementations, notably Ingres, System R, SQL Server, Oracle, and, with delay, IBM's DB2.[1]

Initially, relational databases focused on transactional processes. Those use cases necessitated data engineering practices like normal forms, notably third normal form (3NF).[2] 3NF focused on eliminating redundancies and repetitions in data. Coherent OnLine Transactional Processes (OLTP) need these rules. The design minimized storage space. With increasing data model volume and complexity, those designs became too slow for OnLine Analytical Processing (OLAP). OLAP necessitated fast processing of substantial amounts of correlated data. There is an even greater demand if data is needed to train machine learning models or feed modern in-memory data visualization and data analysis tools.[3] These tools require integrated data in large quantities.[4]

---

[1] History of databases from the Computer History Museum. https://www.youtube.com/watch?v=KG-mqHoXOXY.

[2] See for example https://en.wikipedia.org/wiki/Third_normal_form.

[3] Tools like QlikSense, PowerBI, Spotfire, and more.

[4] The term "analytics" is used very loosely. "Analytics" serves as a proxy for the entire range of data visualization, data analytics, data science, the entire span from descriptive to diagnostic to predictive to prescriptive analytics including data provisioning for training and executing machine learning models.

This led to OLAP and OLTP as distinct design paradigms. Differentiated technologies emerged beyond the traditional row-based relational databases, including various variants of NoSQL databases. Those technologies mostly process unstructured or semi-structured data.[5]

This book focuses on OLAP data model design enabling modular, coherent, flexible datamarts, data lakehouses, and data pipelines. We can compare the approach in this book to star schema or snowflake models on steroids. These designs focus on the needs of large, diverse, and complex enterprises. It is hard to beat physics. These simplified marts rely on new database technologies, such as columnar stores to handle some of the resulting complexities. These are key for making simplified models practical and realistic.

The resulting pragmatic and generic models described in this book enable enterprise data marts to grow with the business, adapt to changing and evolving needs, and integrate data irrespective of source system, technology, function, convention, or data life cycle.[6] The modularity ensures flexibility regarding business questions, and the precise business question does not need to be known in advance and can change over time.

Figure 2: Artistic representation of integrated marts. Illustration created with https://kumu.io

---

[5] See https://www.jesse-anderson.com/2022/12/brief-history-of-data-engineering/.

[6] The terms enterprise data mart and enterprise data model are used interchangeably across many sections in this book. There is little value for having a model without it being implemented somewhere, made usable and accessible. On the other hand, one cannot implement a usable, extensible mart without having a model.

# Data warehouse / lake / data lakehouse

"Enterprise Data Model" is the oldest term in this context. Let's briefly look at its definition before looking at others. *"An enterprise data model is a type of data model that presents a view of all data consumed across the organization. It provides an integrated yet broad overview of the enterprise's data, regardless of the data management technology used."*[7]

Now let's look at other terms. There are many definitions of data lake and data warehouse. Wikipedia states, *"a data lake is a system or repository of data stored in its natural/raw format, usually object blobs or files. A data lake is usually a single store of data including raw copies of source system data, sensor data, social data etc., and transformed data."*[8] while a data warehouse has processed data for a purpose. Others[9] state that a data warehouse is ETL (extract transform load) while a data lake is ELT (extract load transform). Others further differentiate a data lake from a data swamp to indicate different levels of data quality. Finally, others again define that a data lake can contain structured and unstructured data while a data warehouse has just structured data.

As you can see, data lake is a very ambiguous term. Later, the term data lakehouse surfaced,[10] which claims to overcome the limitations of both a data lake and a data warehouse while maintaining the qualities of each and providing analytic flexibility. In this book, we use the term [enterprise] data lakehouse. Our modular data lakehouse is neither a data lake nor a data dump. Instead, it is a deliberately crafted set of mini-marts. Mini-marts are our elementary building blocks, the "objects" that are combined to address specific business questions. They are comparable to the Data Quantum in Zhamak Dehghani's book on Data Mesh, although they might not be as comprehensive.

Our data lakehouse is multipurpose. While it is implemented and funded with a set of initial business questions in mind, it is not limited to these questions. The detailed business questions can but need not be known in advance. The modular mini-marts are elementary and standardized. Mini-marts are facts, pure data at the finest granularity without interpretation. Only the intrinsic knowledge pertinent to the respective source systems and processes is embedded in mini-marts. They can be combined and assembled freely to address new and changing requirements.

---

[7] https://www.techopedia.com/definition/30596/enterprise-data-model.

[8] https://en.wikipedia.org/wiki/Data_lake.

[9] E.g. https://www.talend.com/resources/data-lake-vs-data-warehouse
https://www.datacamp.com/blog/data-lakes-vs-data-warehouses
https://www.guru99.com/data-lake-vs-data-warehouse.html.

[10] https://www.databricks.com/glossary/data-lakehouse.

## Star and snowflake models

We design star and Snowflake models to overcome the limitations of normalized OLTP models. Analytic use cases often need large amounts of data in different combinations. Star and snowflake models replace the complex joins inherent in most OLTP models with simplified fact tables containing the measures and relations to dimensions, either one-level, the star models, or multi-level, snowflake models. They allow efficient retrieval of large amounts of data. While the dimensions tell you *what* it is, facts tell you *how much*. Helena Nacinovic, Digital Learning Manager for SAP HANA Cloud, defines dimensions as "*... pieces of data that allow you to understand and index measures in your data models. Dimensions are either characteristic of a measure or pieces of data that help contextualize the fact.*"[11]

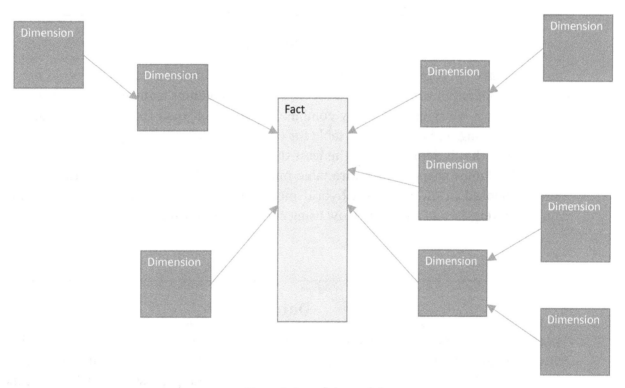

Figure 3: Snowflake model

Additional concepts include slowly changing dimensions, snapshot tables, and data vaults. The techniques outlined in this book provide functionality for changing dimension, whether slowly changing or fast, for data historicization and for snapshot tables and avoid the complexities of a data vault. They focus on the question, "How to enable integrated enterprise data at scale such that we can combine it into myriads of different combinations, addressing a wide range of business questions."

---

[11] https://blogs.sap.com/2021/07/22/facts-measures-and-dimensions.

Although we circumvent the complexities of slowly changing dimensions and data vaults, we extend on conformed dimensions. Using the definition from techtarget.com: *"In data warehousing, a conformed dimension is a dimension that has the same meaning to every fact with which it relates. Conformed dimensions allow facts and measures to be categorized and described in the same way across multiple facts and/or data marts, ensuring consistent reporting across the enterprise."*[12]

Conformed dimensions allow data reuse across different marts. In this book, we build on them, disambiguate them and incorporate synonyms to make them practical in complex, historically grown multi-system environments.

## Full denormalization

Some data lake concepts simply use fully denormalized huge flat tables. They do not rely on snowflakes but rather combine facts with "all relevant" columns from dimensions, thus avoiding any joins when querying data. They combine "all relevant" data from customers or materials into one big, long, and broad "lake" table for each individual sales transaction. There are many challenges with this approach, not the least the definition of "all relevant." If any of those "all relevant" columns change, the entire table must be reloaded. For this and other reasons, the model proposed in the book is a hybrid model, a snowflake model on steroids, suited for complex enterprises as outlined below using controlled denormalizations.

## Data load

There are various design methodologies and techniques for getting data into the lakehouse. Sometimes there is also a differentiation between ETL (Extract, Transform, and Load) versus ELT (Extract, Load, Transform). Both versions describe the process for getting the data from the source into the data marts. This process can be done regularly, such as hourly, daily, or continuously, depending on the business requirements, data volumes, technology, and business needs. The latter (ELT) is sometimes more flexible. The schema needed to address the business question is only defined after the load. Hence, it is easier to adapt to new and changing requirements.

We take a hybrid approach in this book. It is ETL to the point of conformed, modular mini-marts, yet those mini-marts do not predefine the schema for query nor constrain the business questions. It builds on established concepts yet simplifies these concepts by:

---

[12] https://www.techtarget.com/searchdatamanagement/definition/conformed-dimension.

- Keeping code complexity low.

- Scaling linearly as the uptake and scope increase.

- Retaining all information from the raw data to the marts.

- Being source system agnostic, generalizing and consolidating data from multiple sources.

- Managing history, irrespective of whether this history changes fast or slowly.

- Enabling transparent lineage information, increasing trust in the data.

- Allowing for full, incremental, or even near-real-time data load.

- Coping with different business calendars and asynchronous business days across geographies and systems.

- Allowing parallel and independent threads for data load.

- Enabling addition/globalization of hard and soft business rules where needed, and localization where appropriate.

---

## The enterprise challenge

We use a model enterprise and its data challenges as an example. Our model enterprise is a mature, established organization. The enterprise is the result of various mergers and acquisitions. Consequentially it has not one but several transactional systems supporting the day-to-day operations. Those systems, often Enterprise Resource Planning (ERP) systems like SAP, Oracle, and many others, might be split by business function, geography, or even merger history. Each of those systems covers parts of the business. Some data is unique. Others might be common across all systems but not necessarily identical. In addition, our model enterprise has different customer relations, marketing, and front-facing systems, potentially split between geography or heritage.

Some of those systems might be fully or partially integrated yet have their own local convention or sales-specific view of customers and their own view of products. For example, marketing might have a different view or focus on products and customers than production and supply. Sometimes data is entered directly to meet the sales' and marketing's viewpoint on how they see "things." This conglomerate of systems is further supported in our model enterprise by local point-of-sale systems and shop-floor controls, budgeting and planning systems, global systems for financial consolidation, costing and reporting, and an abundance of different systems used in Research and Development (R&D). Consequently, different systems might use different identifiers for the same or different customers, products, and organizations. Product identification changes along the product life cycle. Development might use a product definition that is different from the one used in marketing. This makes it difficult to accomplish an end-to-end view.

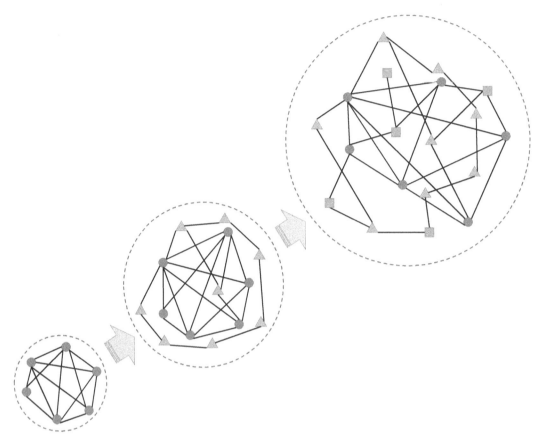

Figure 4: Evolution of enterprise complexity

Our model enterprise relies on integrated data. Sometimes that data is provided by a truly integrated data warehouse. Sometimes this integration is achieved by downloading individual data sets, reports, or tables from various sources. This integration is sometimes automated and then combined at report time. Often those data downloads are specific to the relevant report/business question at hand, heavily using tools like Excel. Multiple parallel downloads might be implemented for the same or slightly different content or viewpoint, leading to ambiguities in KPIs reported and the proliferation of similar information, often in the form of sharing Excel files. Besides being confusing, it is inefficient, labor-intensive, and time-consuming. Getting a true 360° view across customers and processes is difficult. This approach poses a substantial entry hurdle to truly agile, explorative data analysis based on integrated data.

We must and can do better. The techniques described here address these challenges in a modular and incremental way.

Our model enterprise guides three aspects of the enterprise datamart. It guides agile, data-driven decision-making, addresses the challenges and demands inherent to our model enterprise, and provides modularity for the enterprise mart. This book addresses the methodologies and techniques, the design guidelines, and the model templates for the marts.

## Agile data-informed decision making

In this chapter, we outline a framework that separates asking the right question from identifying the data needed and then analyzing that data.

To address the topic, we look first at what enables agility in data-driven decision making. To understand what this means, we look at a data-informed decision framework. Although there are many decision-making frameworks, we will use the one in Figure 5.[13]

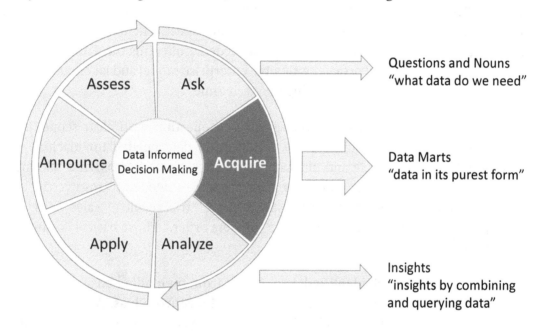

Figure 5: Framework for data-informed decision making

The cycle starts with

1. "Ask". The "What", the question to address. It must be clear, specific, scoped, and answerable.

2. "Acquire". Acquire the data needed, the nouns. These are the core of our approach. They define "what we need to know" to answer a question and ultimately define the mini-marts.

---

[13] adapted from https://thedataliteracyproject.org/ and Qlik's content for data literacy in their Continuous Classroom for Data Literacy.

3. "Analyze". Combine, appraise and analyze the data from various sources.

4. "Apply". Integrate the data and insights with professional expertise. Be conscious of implied bias. Every insight leads to new or revised questions. Sometimes the cycle stops here and we start over again unless the initial results look promising.

5. "Announce". Decide, and communicate.

6. "Assess". Monitor the outcome.

Steps 1 through 4 are often repeated multiple times. The more agile we are, the quicker that cycle and the faster we can gain insights and fine-tune our actions.

The nouns are a main output of "Ask." They are the basic business facts needed to answer the question. They define "what we need to know to answer the question." Asking the right questions is an art whereby a data lakehouse cannot assist. The data lakehouse accelerates the subsequent step, "acquire," collecting the data needed. Collecting the data is often the proverbial iceberg in any data-focused project. A flexible enterprise model and lakehouse shortens the time needed to acquire data, thus shortening the cycle time.

The Ask Cycle must formulate a precise, focused question with clear scope, independent of whether it is a business inquiry or the definition of data needed for machine learning. This question will drive the cycle and ultimately provide a set of "Verbs" and "Nouns." The Verbs and Nouns are the basic data objects or their properties needed to resolve the question. Such basic data or nouns can be "inventory," "sales orders," "trial results," "sales plans," "cost of goods sold," "page visits," or complex objects like "process order." Those basic data objects later define the mini-marts.

It is critical to isolate such identified data objects from their allied business interpretations and assumptions to enable these objects complete and free from bias. Assumptions behind those data objects must be made explicit within the data objects. Business interpretations are added later in the "analyze" step.

# One

# Enterprise Data Lakehouse Overview

This chapter looks at the modular nature of the marts and addresses data mesh and demand management. The subsequent chapter will cover the principles behind the mini-marts followed by detailed design standards.

## Modular data marts

A business question is often a series of facts and rules strung together in specific ways. These "data journeys" address specific questions, combining information in relation to each other. For example, a question can be, "What were the properties of components used in products that we sold mostly to customers in a specific region?"

In the introduction, we saw how to ask precise business questions to identify the "nouns." Many different business questions need the same nouns. Each of those "nouns," such as "properties," "components," "products," "sales," "customers," and "regions" become individual data objects or mini-marts. We shall first address those individual elements, the mini-marts, and then see how to string them together. We will explain mini-marts using a sales order and later return to our product properties and components example.

The business question might ask about the details of a sales order. To answer that question, one needs a complete statement such as "Sales order 721634, created on December 12 2023, for customer number 11, which is MyCustomer, and shipped to customer number 23, which is MyCustomer's warehouse in Winslow, is approved and contains four materials, one of them 200 items of material number 34A which are tea kettles of which the first 100 will ship on Dec 20."

Looking at the individual nouns, we get three mini-marts. The one for customer informs us that 11 is MyCustomer and 23 is his warehouse in Winslow. The one for material tells us that 34A are tea kettles and other information such as household goods. The mini-mart for sales order tells us that order 721634, created Dec 12 2023, sold to 11, shipped to 23, approved, one of four materials is 34A, 200 of them, 100 of them shipped on Dec 20, and more information such as further shipments and the details of the other materials ordered. So we have three mini-marts: customer, material, and sales order.

We'll have many such mini-marts in our complex enterprise. So let's see how we cope with new and changing business questions, how we can construct those mini-marts in such a way that we do not need to know the precise business question in advance, and in such a manner that we can string them together in many different ways to address different business questions.

To illustrate the above, we could use the analogy of a toy railway. In our toy railway analogy, the mini-marts are the basic objects and are represented by the individual railway track pieces (the straight, curved, long, short tracks). An individual business question can be seen as a journey, starting with a piece of knowledge or data and then traveling from one piece of related knowledge to the next one until we reach the destination. To do this, we assemble the individual marts in specific ways to address the business questions. The railway track pieces can connect to each other because they all adhere to the same rules on how they connect. These rules will later become the common dimensions, the disambiguated natural business keys. Later on, we'll see what "disambiguation" means in detail. Answering specific questions means stringing the tracks together and "traveling" from one object or "piece of knowledge" to the next. This is a "data journey," traveling from one piece of information to related pieces of information. There are many such journey possible.

Let's use an illustration. We receive complaints from one of our customer's headquarters about product quality. We also have the test results from the suppliers of the components we purchase. We want to know which components were in the products we shipped to this customer and the Supplier Test results for these specific components. A good business question here, for example, would be, "Is there a correlation between test results and headquarters complaints?"

We need to string the individual pieces of information together to address this question. We must be able to "travel" from one piece of knowledge to the next, so they must be connected.[14] We start with the test results that we receive from the components supplier. Those tests are identified by the product number used by the supplier, so we need to translate or travel from the supplier's product number into our own. Next, we need to know which products we produced using those components. This information might be in bill of materials. These can be recursive if the components are used in subassemblies for the final product. We sell the labeled product to customers. Our logistics systems define these customers by the logistics systems-generated customer number. This customer number is not necessarily the same as the one used in marketing systems for various reasons. Therefore we need to find the corresponding customer number as used in marketing. The customer might be a large organization with

---

[14] The example is for illustration only. It makes assumptions about business processes that are not universal. It assumes the supplier and your enterprise use different identifiers for the same material/component or that we maintain customer hierarchies in the marketing system. These assumptions might be right or wrong (likely wrong), yet they help illustrating the journey.

headquarters, regional offices, branches, and local stores. Even though we shipped to branches or local stores, we received complaints directly from the headquarters or regional office. Therefore we need to find all branches and stores that belong to this headquarter or regional office. These stores are the relevant ones for which we need to analyze the initial test results of the components of the products we delivered to these stores.

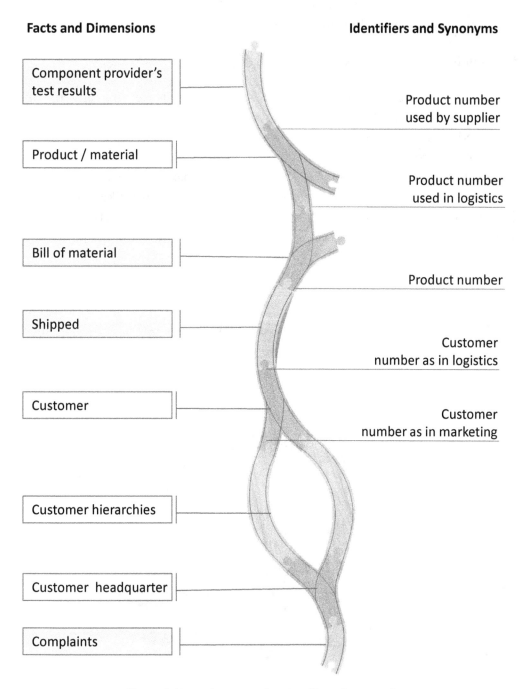

Figure 6: Example connecting data like railway tracks

Building on the toy railway analogy, this is a data journey. Mini-marts can easily help us make this data journey. To do this, we build on specific capabilities fundamental to our mini-marts. We will learn about them in detail in the next chapter:

- Dimensions with synonyms help us get the supplier's and our product numbers for materials and a customer's related numbers as used in logistics and marketing. These dimensions have flexible hierarchies, like the relationship between headquarters, regional offices, branches, and local stores.

- Facts are other things we know, such as the components' test results, bill of materials, shipping information, and complaints.

We combine the mini-marts for exactly that question.

Any other statement, such as, "Which sales-person is serving any of this organization's headquarters branch offices?" would be a different journey, using some mini-marts we used above and some new ones. Either are using the features and capabilities inherent to any mini-mart. More systematically, how we connect these objects leads to the object model needed to address this specific question. We can combine a basic set of elementary tracks into many different trails, each one addressing a business question. This is like words in a natural language. Simple questions are short sentences, while more complex questions require more of those objects.

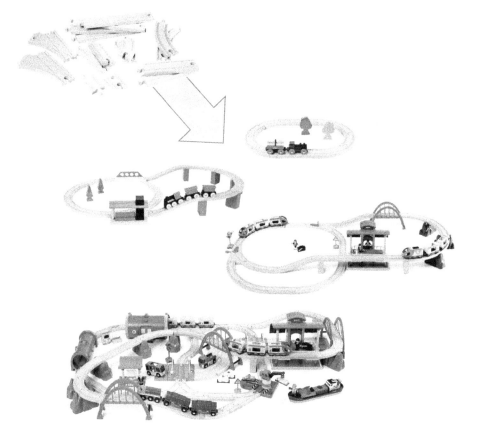

Figure 7: Assembling complex solutions from simple parts[15]

---

[15] courtesy of BRIO AB, Malmö, Sweden.

Here is another example. Assume you sell seeds. You want to sell the best seeds to maximize yield and income for a farmer. The yield depends heavily on weather, soil type, and other parameters. New seeds were bred and tested under different conditions at various locations. Advising a farmer for the best seeds for their location needs comparing conditions at the farmer's location with the conditions and results obtained during breeding. In short, we need to compare weather and other parameters where the seeds were tested with the weather where the final product will be planted. To do this, the analyst "travels" from the weather statistics at a customer's location to the product they purchased, to the components of this product, the trials done while developing the product and finally to the weather data and other parameters relevant for this trial's location. In short, you associate the weather statistics from the customer with the weather statistics and trial results. To do this, you stitch together a few tracks (our nouns), such as weather, location, customer, product, component, trial, and trial outcome.

We can also see those as tiles that fit together in many combinations.

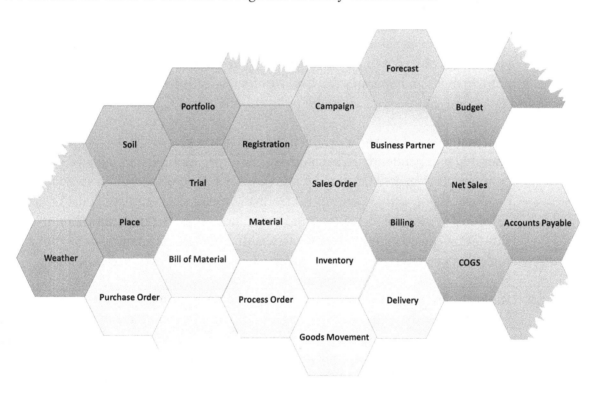

Figure 8: A representation of mini-marts as tiles

We don't dwell on domain-driven data management, although it becomes obvious that any mini-marts belong to one or multiple domains. Each mini-mart can be treated individually. They can be created, extended, and integrated across multiple domains.

## Data mesh

The linear complexity and continuous scaling of the mini-marts simplify the data mesh. This book focuses on the design and computational aspects of such an integrated, potentially federated approach and does not claim to address all socio-technical aspects. It excludes product versus project thinking, decentralizing data ownership and team structures, DevOps, and other aspects of data mesh. The book focuses on the independence and interoperability of the mini-marts which are a key requirement for a successful data mesh. It enables sharing joint information while giving each "node" or domain in the mesh autonomy over the information it "owns" and contributes.

The techniques presented in this book do not rely on co-located data. Mini-marts can be distributed across the various nodes of a data mesh. The following properties and characteristics of the mini-marts enable the data mesh:

- **Independence of mini-marts**. Enables creating mini-marts independently from each other while still enabling data integration and data sharing across domains. Each domain owns and operates the data for the respective domain. The integration across the various domains is facilitated by using synonyms and common dimensions.

- **Independence of workflows**. Even individual workflows can be implemented and operated independently of each other. Therefore multiple domains can contribute to common mini-marts. This can be relevant for shared objects such as a consolidated product catalog with its synonyms from all domains, a joint list of customers with their respective synonym identifiers, and other basic objects. Such unified mini-marts are substantially easier for consumers to use than sets of fragmented or partial mini-marts. It also reduces the risk that a mini-mart's design diverges across domains.

- **Inherent use of synonyms**. Different data domains or mesh nodes might use different identifiers for the same "thing." The inherent use of synonyms in dimensions enables multiple contributors to the same mini-mart. It enables sharing data across domains even if they commonly use different identifiers, which often happens in mature organizations. It allows adding additional synonyms or correcting mistaken synonyms without affecting the data we already have in any mesh node.

- **Shared data catalog, including reserved columns and common dimensions**. The data catalog has an unambiguous list of common dimensions and rules for disambiguating identifiers and defines columns with common meanings across all mini-marts. This list allows each domain within the mesh to act independently while jointly contributing to the list of common terms.

# Demand management

Mini-marts forestall that each project has to pull the data individually from the source systems. The mini-marts are created in place of each project retrieving data individually. Demand management orchestrates the creation and maintenance of those mini-marts. The initial creation of a modular mini-mart is driven by a business case needing specific data. Yet they are implemented for use beyond the initial use case. Mini-marts are implemented following common standards and methodologies. They become part of the reusable data infrastructure or data pipelines. This has several advantages:

- **Agility**. The mini-mart captures the pure, undiluted business facts and transforms them into an easy-to-consume form. Moreover, the data collected is not limited to this initial business need. This allows iterating, refining, and revising the business question in fast cycles.

- **Reusability and flexibility**. Almost every question leads to a new one. Therefore, re-iterating data acquisition for every variation of the business question leads to additional costs. Designing the mini-marts as described allows reusing them for broadly related business questions without the risk of repeating data acquisition.

- **Extensibility**. Business questions tend to grow, asking for a bigger scope. The generic, source-system agnostic design of the mini-marts inherently supports this growth. Adding more data into the same generic structure becomes natural. There is no rework of an existing investment. It avoids parallel data universes and data pipelines, thus saving costs.

The haste to deliver might stipulate supposedly simple solutions focusing on a specific use case with "one-off" exports into spreadsheets. These might be slightly faster for the initial data preparation and showcase delivery.[16] This initial advantage is soon lost if the business requirements are refined or the solution must be sustainably automated. The advantages completely vanish as soon as one intends to use the same data for a different use case or as soon as one assumes reusability of the data. Although data is just pure business facts and usage agnostic, someone asked for it first. This might lead to "discussions" once the same data is needed for a different use case in another function or worse, if we need to extend the data, integrating another data source. There might be a tendency to avoid using the data as it "belongs to someone else" and is "too cumbersome for me to ask for permission to extend it."

Organizations must avoid the tendency to "guard" their data and incentivize reuse. We must incentify the data lakehouse delivery organization to extend existing mini-marts irrespective of original ownership. The organization must support shared ownership and mini-mart evolution

---

[16] Not incentivizing the short-sighted one-off solution is often tricky. One needs to look behind shiny façades to uncover hidden technical debt and lock-in.

to reap the benefits of an integrated data universe. The undesired alternative is parallel variations of almost the same data fragmented across the organization.

# Two

# Design Principles

This chapter discusses what it takes for an enterprise data model to facilitate an enterprise data lakehouse. Our enterprise data model and the resulting lakehouse must integrate data across the enterprise's entire technology, process, systems, and business landscape. Integrating data is substantially more than just collecting source data in one place. The enterprise data lakehouse must be more than a data swamp.

A usable enterprise data lakehouse provides:

- **Versatility**. It is not limited to business questions being known in advance and is open for agile data exploration beyond the initial use case. It explores and uses data in different combinations for different purposes in an agile, collaborative, iterative way.

- **Accessibility**. It mitigates the challenge of complex application logic. The data is documented, accessible, and interpretable by users not familiar with the original source systems and their embedded implicit assumptions.

- **Flexibility**. It integrates data from "anywhere" with "anything." Different "data objects" can integrate irrespective of source system and other former constraints. The user does not need to know specifics of any source system to integrate or combine its data with data from another source.

- **Findability**. Identifies the relevant data. "Find" it intuitively by various search criteria. Data can be found and identified independent of the source system or data owner.

## Preamble

The approach presented here became realistic only in the last few years. Although the approach is technology independent, its implementation and simplification rely on newer database concepts unavailable when alternate approaches were first proposed. The approach is made feasible with the emergence of columnar databases for large data volumes. They enable sparsely populated tables and compress repeating content resulting from denormalizations and other simplifications. Those simplifications make the approach scalable and, most importantly, make the data understandable and consumable for self-service and exploration. The examples used in this book build on a single database. While this simplifies the examples, it is not a prerequisite. The techniques and methodologies can be implemented with a singular database or using a data mesh. Furthermore, de-coupled processes lend themselves well to a federated data mesh approach. It is not about technology. It is about what the data tells us and how it fits together.

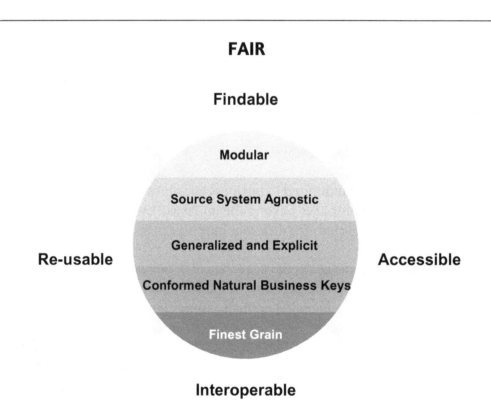

Figure 9: Basic principles of modular mini-marts

The FAIR principles [Findable, Accessible, Interoperable, and Reusable] [17] are well established. The mini-marts build and extend on them. There is one key difference, though. Our mini-marts must serve the complexities of our model enterprise with all its ambiguities, synonyms, and partially overlapping data. Therefore, the very first principle for findable is extended. The original principle states, "*Data is assigned a globally unique and persistent identifier.*" Instead of "a globally ... identifier," the sentence should state "one or more" globally persistent identifiers. We'll see the detail of this in this chapter and more about natural business keys and synonyms in dimensions.

---

[17] Amongst other sources, *https://en.wikipedia.org/wiki/FAIR_data.*

Let's now look at the details of the mini-marts that enable them to be FAIR even in our complex and dynamic environment.

Accessible and Findable can be seen in two ways: From "having the right tool" to access data and from "understandable data structure and content." Having the right tools to access data is very individual and certainly driven by factors outside the scope of this book. This book addresses how to create understandable data structure and content, including data catalogs.

Obviously, an enterprise data lakehouse must be adopted and used to provide value. Adoption will only occur if using the data is easy—if a user does not need to know the details of every source system. Accessibility goes beyond system independent. For example, a module in SAP can easily have hundreds of tables. Building a custom report that pulls in data from several tables in a database can only be done by a team member who knows how to query a database using SQL or another specialized query language. Such data is only accessible to someone who knows the technical details of the respective source application. Once they've surfaced the requested data, that person might format the data into something more digestible for the intended audience or pass that duty along to another team member. An earlier example was used about sales orders where 100 tea kettles were shipped on Dec 20. From this description, we can infer that the question has at least five tables in the transactional source system:

- A table for customers [11 is MyCustomer and 23 his warehouse].

- A table for the materials [34A is tea kettles].

- A table for header [order 721634, created Dec 12, 2023, sold to 11, shipped to 23, approved].

- A table containing each line item or material [200 items of 34A].

- Finally, a table for the individual shipments [100 of 34A shipped on Dec 20].

To extract the complete business knowledge of a sales order, you need to know how the individual tables join and what logic to apply for interpreting the data. We also do not want to do full denormalization for reasons explained before. From the five tables above, we can derive three mini-marts, two simple ones for customer and material and one more complex one for sales order. You can only know the business meaning of a sales order once you completely understand the tables for a sales order's header, line item, and shipping quantity and how they connect.

Accessibility is more than having technical and organizational access. It means simplifications and ease of understanding relevant data without needing to know the internals of the source system(s). Our data marts must be oriented along the business meaning in user terms, not by source technology or topology. We need to access data without knowing the intrinsic detail of source tables and the internal logic. A truly accessible mini-mart simplifies the data into its pure business meaning. Those descriptions only use business terms, no technical table names, column names, or tech jargon. The answer is a simple business statement.

Interoperable and reusable means that design and implementation of the enterprise data lakehouse with its mini-marts can be done before and without knowing all business questions that will be asked.

The mini-marts must have common "connectors" to be interoperable. Common connectors help us connect almost every mini-mart with every other one. Or, to build on the railway analogy, we can connect those tracks in many ways because all adhere to the same rules for connecting by having compatible connectors between them.

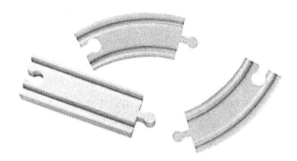

Figure 10: Railway track example of matching connectors

Similarly, the mini-marts forming the data lakehouse must meet certain conditions and principles. Those enable combining the mini-marts for any business question we want to address. They are interoperable and re-usable. Those conditions are:

- **Modular**. We can implement and test each mini-mart independently of any other, curbing complexity and enabling fast implementation and quick time to deliver. The mini-marts for sales orders, materials, customers, trials, or any other, can be implemented or enhanced independently from the other by different teams. Their implementation or enhancement does not depend on each other.

- **Source system agnostic**. A mini-mart is source system agnostic. The same mini-mart can combine data from multiple sources.

- **Finest grain**. Mini-marts contain the data at the finest, original granularity available in the source systems. Aggregation comes after. The mini-mart for sales order in our tea kettle example contains each individual sales order, line items, and reference to deliveries. Data in the mini-mart is not aggregated, even though one report will later aggregate per material group or per customer.

- **Generalized and explicit**. Each mini-mart consolidates different "flavors" or types of the same kind of data, providing all the relevant information. However, there's no implicit meaning in the data. Our earlier example on sales order was implicitly about direct sales (we sold). Indirect sales data is similar, so we can generalize both into the same mini-mart and explicitly indicate the type of sales the seller made. Similarly, materials can contain all materials from all regions, whether in early research, in production, or even just for promotion purposes.

- **Conformed natural business keys.** We use natural business keys to join mini-marts together. These are disambiguated and aligned to act as conformed dimensions. Customer 752445 might be Jones LLP in the transactional system used for Europe, yet the same customer number 752445 might be Vaso Artesano in the system used for sales processes in the Americas while marketing processes use 00x23rtA as the customer number for Vaso Artesano.

## Modular

Reusing data yields the biggest savings. The data is modular. Reusability is not only a technical question but also an organizational challenge. Sometimes there's a mental hurdle, especially in large organizations with a strong project focus. Mini-marts get created because of a business need. Often those business needs result in projects. Addressing a business need sometimes requires data not yet available. Hence integrating new data, creating a new mini-mart is almost always initiated by a project or use case. Projects have a limited budget. Individual projects have little incentive to think beyond their immediate data needs and create the mini-marts in a reusable way. Yet the bigger enterprise benefits greatly if subsequent projects do not need to start from scratch. Rather they can reuse what has been created before. Therefore, the greater enterprise benefits if individual projects create the mini-marts in a comprehensive and reusable way.

Achieving reusability and modularity needs minimal governance and management support. We've seen above why projects create data silos to address their immediate needs. Many of us have seen those ubiquitous Excel sheets. This forces other projects to do the same. It results in a proliferation of different marts with similar yet slightly different data and a loss of transparency about which mart contains what. Designing for reusability is inexpensive. It is achieved through upfront design principles, standardization, and how-to guides. It avoids re-invention. It benefits the entire organization. Common rules and a common data catalog are a starting point for governance. Incentives for reuse can be achieved if the data is sold as a product where reuse lowers the costs of serving multiple customers. Alternatively, reuse is incentivized if a larger data and analytics organizational unit serves various customers' needs. Such an organization is incentivized to reduce its overall costs and time for delivery. It will be incentivized to invest a little more upfront in data acquisition as it pays back multiple times for subsequent needs. The last alternative, which is forcing reuse by decree, is seldom effective.

Either of these approaches, whether data as a product or owned by a common organization, leads to business use cases driving the priority of the mini-mart implementation. We implement the mini-marts with a bigger mindset. They are independent of use case and can be used beyond the initial use case. They contain the complete data from the source.

Each mini-mart has clear business content and broad scope. Often initial data is confined to the immediate need due to legacy thinking. We can do better. Including all entries from the same source into a mini-mart is not substantially more expensive than adding a subset of the entries. It is just more of the same, removing filters. Yet including all entries benefits everybody. One can iterate much faster on its front-end. Mini-marts contain the complete set of "rows" available. They do not apply filters or implied business assumptions and contain the full set of columns available.

Modularity helps the mini-marts to be interoperable and re-usable. Yet it is not only about modularity itself. Complexity grows as we add more modules. A traditional data warehouse's complexity, cost, and inertia tend to rapidly inflate as content expands. We can break this trend provided we make the cost for adding additional components or objects independent of the number of objects already existing. Implementing changes to any mini-mart must not be negatively affected by any existing marts beyond agreeing on standards early.

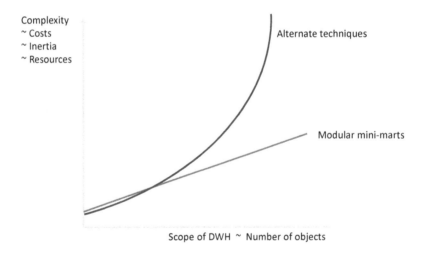

Figure 11: Linear vs. exponential growth

Linear growth can be achieved by throwing several old principles overboard, like unique keys in all cases, by using GUIDs[18] only within and not between mini-marts, and by building all relations on natural business keys, disambiguated where needed. Further down, we'll see that this adds to the simplicity and to the marts' trust and transparency. In addition, it enables an asynchronous and transparent approach to data quality. This approach satisfies both, the viewpoint of the creator of the data and the different viewpoints users have when using and combining data beyond their initial purpose.

---

[18] GUID: Globally Unique Identifier.

Independent mini-marts simplify project management, eliminating cross dependencies, allowing project teams or their data mesh domains to work largely independently from each other. To summarize, mini-marts can and are implemented and enhanced independent of each other.

## System agnostic

The mini-marts must be agnostic and independent of the system they are sourced from. For example, R&D systems, marketing services, production, and supply each have their own view and knowledge of looking at a "material" along the product life cycle. All these sources contribute to the same data object for "material" and collectively enrich it. Such generalization and consolidation are possible for sales data from different regional systems, even for direct and indirect sales, for inventory, marketing activity data, etc.

Similar business facts from different source systems are consolidated into one mini-mart, further tearing down boundaries between systems. We shall see more about this in the chapter about generalization. Each mini-mart can contain data from multiple sources. It can contain data from the various regional transactional systems or even internal and external sources combined.

The technical source system does not guide the rules for consolidation. A mini-mart should therefore never be named after a source system. Neither should the habitual naming of things limit consolidation. Mini-marts consolidate along common business meanings. Extracting the precise business meaning is sometimes a tricky endeavor. Later, we'll use the stem "This row tells me....."

Segregation between "things" is deeply embedded in business practice, resulting in different naming of things that are conceptually similar, if not identical. The system-agnostic implementation and consolidation require an open mind. It requires focusing on business meaning versus the technology source. While the mini-marts have consolidated data, the different source systems and subtypes are made explicit in each mini-mart. Different sources and subtypes translate into explicit content in columns like record_type and/or source_system.

Mini-marts must rely only on data officially exposed by the source system, data representing the business meaning. Refrain from using internal technical keys outside the respective source system, as it would create hard dependencies between systems and limit the abilities of either system to evolve independently.

Consolidating multiple sources into the same mini-mart is often a shift in thinking for some traditional developers. They are used to a system-specific representation of data. Two major arguments exist in the discussion of how mini-marts are generalized and source system agnostic.

- **The first of these arguments is "The business calls it differently."** Different business-specific languages for the same thing. Similar things are called differently. For example, account in marketing versus customer for sales data. This is a typical illustration where marketing talks of an account while sales uses the term customer. They can be different persona for the same party. Others might call a batch that's sampled for quality testing an inspection lot while it is a sub-batch or a sample elsewhere. While both are correct, they are closely related if not the same thing. Consolidating data into one mini-mart and, at the same time, disambiguating the meaning creates clarity and simplifies using the data. It is a departure from habitual behavior. It has the biggest impact on reducing the number of objects in the first place, making the entire data lakehouse easier to navigate and more generic to use.

- **The second argument is where "different things" with the same business meaning might have attributes or properties that are only partially overlapping.** We might know 20 columns for one "subtype of a thing" and we might know 10 common and 20 other columns for another "subtype of the same thing". In the past, these were stored in different physical tables or marts or supported by elaborate normalized models. This made integration cumbersome or changes complex. Yet there's a different viewpoint. Each property tells us something we "know about it." Having the combination of all available columns in the mini-mart while just populating those properties for which there is information currently available makes the entire object more generic, simpler to use, and easier to extend. Modern technologies (columnar stores) can deal with the resulting sparsely populated tables.

To summarize, the data in the mini-marts has aligned business meaning irrespective of their technical source. Multiple sources can and will be combined. The source systems are visible and explicit via audit-column.

## Finest grain

Data granularity is the level of detail of a data set. More granular data can provide more detailed analysis and be more precise.[19] If we cannot answer a question with the finest grain of data available, then you must rephrase the question or find more data.

Aggregations vary, are often determined and filtered by additional data like a product's status or a customer's rating, and are never what's required for this specific analysis unless there is a proliferation of similar data in slightly different aggregations and interpretations. This is not an ideal solution.

---

[19] Rkimball.com.

Modern systems are powerful enough to handle aggregations dynamically where the number of rows stays below a few billion. This allows keeping the mini-marts at the finest grain. It enables on-demand combining, aggregating, and filtering of data in any way and shape, precisely the way the business question at hand demands. It gives the greatest flexibility in deriving features for machine learning and AI model execution.

To summarize, data in mini-marts is as fine grain as the original source permits. A mini-mart does not loose information previously contained in its source.

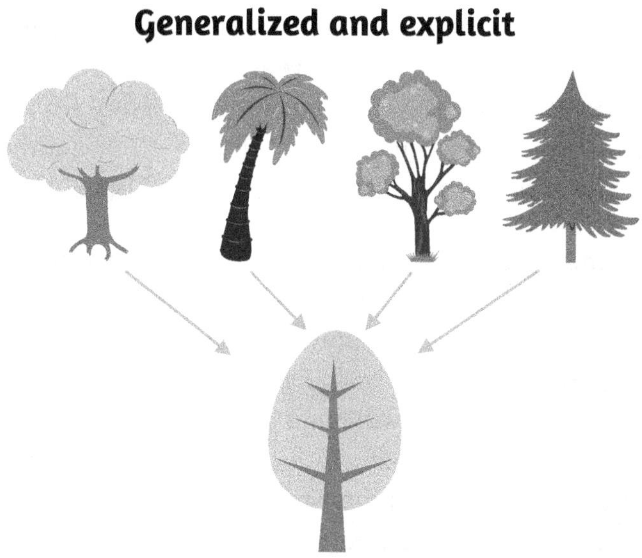

## Generalized and explicit

Figure 12: Generalization

*"A generalization is a form of abstraction whereby common properties of specific instances are formulated as general concepts or claims. Generalizations posit the existence of a domain or set of elements and one or more common characteristics shared by those elements."*[20]

Each mini-mart is atomic, highly generalized, and their relationships are based on natural business keys. Those can be disambiguated where needed.

Atomic is defined as *"of or forming a single irreducible unit or component in a larger system"*[21]: A mini-mart is always consistent within itself. This will become especially relevant when we address repeating entries in dimensions or multi-layered facts.

---

[20] https://en.wikipedia.org/wiki/Generalization.

[21] https://www.encyclopedia.com/science-and-technology/physics/physics/atomic.

Generalized is defined as *"a general statement or concept obtained by inference from specific cases."*[22] Slicing something generic into pieces later is always easier than combining disparate pieces into a generic solution later. Hence, we aim for generic solutions and attempt to generalize and subtype in case of doubt. Examples are the many different types of customers, vendors, materials, organizational units, etc.

There can be many transactional systems having the same or similar data. We generalize and consolidate those in the mini-marts. Each mini-mart is highly generalized and consolidates data from multiple source systems. In the illustration (Fig. Figure 12: Generalization above), we create a mini-mart "tree" for all different types of trees. These generalized mini-marts include all different types of an object and have distinct advantages.

It is easier for data users to identify the generalized mini-mart [like tree or businesspartner] and then differentiate the subtypes. The different subtypes within a mini-mart are made explicit with a dedicated column like record_type. This indicates whether this tree is a pine-tree or whether this business_partner or persona is a prospect, thereby reducing the number of mini-marts and helping with clarity and chasing for "similar things."

Generalization simplifies queries. Identifying the joins between mini-marts is often one of the more mysterious or daunting tasks in real-life environments. The fewer mini-marts there are, the fewer different joins are needed and, therefore, we gain clarity and simplicity. We'll see later how this is simplified using naming conventions for common dimensions. Joins between mini-marts remain unchanged as we adapt the queries for different subtypes, increasing the versatility of any query to scale across different subtypes. However, not all joins might be applicable to all subtypes. This would mean more outer joins. Fortunately, these do not impose the same performance penalty in modern database systems as with older technologies.

Rigorous generalization, in turn, simplifies data lifecycle management. For example, when a customer changes from prospect to verified customer. There is no need to remove the entry from the mini-mart prospect and add it to the mini-mart customer. Instead, updating the record_type or the persona in the mini-mart business_partners from prospect to customer suffices. Later we shall explore more elaborate schemas using the party concept with personas.

Generalization is only possible if all implicit context and assumptions are made explicit. Filenames or source systems often have implicit meanings for a user of the data. For example, filenames might indicate the country where the data originates from or the creation date. That information is made explicit in the mini-marts. They have dedicated columns for implicit meaning that's hidden in source system properties or other circumstantial information. The mini-marts must carry explicit columns for information such as country or recordingdate. And

---

[22] "generalization ." The Oxford Pocket Dictionary of Current English. Retrieved December 20, 2023, from Encyclopedia.com: https://www.encyclopedia.com/humanities/dictionaries-thesauruses-pictures-and-press-releases/generalization.

dates are explicit, not "previous year" and "current year." Any data can be interpreted without needing implicit information.

A mini-mart in our enterprise model is NOT a raw 1:1 copy of source tables. A mini-mart is not a report either. It is not an interpretation of data and does not have an implicit assumption.

- The finest granularity and easy combination of mini-marts mitigate the proliferation of marts due to different aggregations.

- Each workflow from a source into a mini-mart is largely independent of each other and, therefore, can be added or modified without impacting other flows. Multiple flows can co-exist. This is a key pre-requisite to consolidation and generalization across the organization.

- It is easier and more transparent for users to see the subtypes of data in a mini-mart at once rather than having to hunt for potential "similar marts" with different structures.

- Columnar store can handle sparsely populated tables. This mitigates the fact that not all sources have the same set of attributes or columns. Not all sources can populate all columns of a mini-mart.

- Consolidating sources into the same marts makes it transparent and easy to extend as more columns get added, or objects get further differentiated.

- Consolidating marts "nudges" the consolidation of column names to their business meaning rather than using technical names.

- Consolidated mart can logically be split into distinct slices. If needed, one can create a dedicated view for individual countries of a consolidated global mart.

- Finally, splitting data later in case it really was a mistake is always easier than consolidating data once they are split.

We have a good understanding of the business content in a mini-mart if we can describe the content of a mini-mart with the stem:

"This record tells me that ........"

This sentence sounds simple yet has proven to be surprisingly tricky. It usually takes three iterations to distill the true essence out of convoluted descriptions with systems, mystical process complexity, and local terminology.

Here are some bad examples:

- "It is the process order from SAPAB" instead of "This record tells me that the production planned for X kg of material A and scheduled to commence on May 3 in plant P needs Y kg of material D. And this record tells me that the production planned for X kg of material A and scheduled to commence on May 3 in plant P will perform painting."

- "These are the sales coming from Point of Sales terminal" instead of "This record tells me that retailer K sold USD Y of product B to customer M who used loyalty card X."

We've seen above that a mini-mart has no implicit assumption. The "knowledge," the data contains no interpretation or implicit business assumptions. In our example, there's no judgement whether 100 tea kettles shipped on Dec 20 is sufficient or whether my customer is a good customer.

Another example is "current budget" and "previous budget." The budget for 2024 is set in May 2023 and another entry is set in July 2023 for 2024. The data in the mini-mart is exactly as stated: budget date and date of budget setting. Classifying entries as "current budget" and "previous budget" is an interpretation of the data. It does not belong in the mini-mart. The most recent budget is interpreted as current, and the previous one as previous. If another budget is defined on Oct 23 for 2024, then the budget from July becomes previous. Hence previous and current is an interpretation of facts, the dates of budget setting are in a classifying column in the mini-mart [May 2023, July 2023, Oct 2023] as is the budget year [2024]. Mistakenly coining business interpretation into mini-marts happen out of habit and legacy ways of working. Sometimes the user's language is so deeply entrenched in the organization that the meaning of it gets lost. Mini-marts contain the meaning, not the interpretation.

Here is a good example:

Inventory: This record tells me that as per last Friday, X quantity of batch Y of product 34A is located in Warehouse 20 and it is free to use. Sales Forecast or planning: one record tells me that sales office Q predicted last week that the consolidated demand for product A in October will be 500 GAL. Or the original customer demand was 700 pieces, and it has been reduced to 550 pieces due to a supply shortage.

Having clarity on what data really means is essential. Good definitions are free of business interpretations. The concepts of hard and soft business rules are used elsewhere in data warehousing concepts. They mean slightly different things. We, therefore, use the terms *physical business rules* and *interpretation business rules*. Physical business rules are reflected when creating the mini-marts, the mini-marts contain the outcome of those rules. Interpretation rules are only applied when using the data. Interpretation rules can change depending on the business question at hand.

Physical business rules interpret the source system's complex structures, making content understandable. They implement how the source system's tables translate into coherent business meaning. They can be technical, such as interpretation of complex relationships between tables and the denormalization of JSONs or XMLs. Physical business rules reflect physical and process business realities like the customer code in a point-of-sales system is derived from those in the transactional system for North America and not from the global system. Collectively, physical business rules replicate what's "hard coded" into the systems and processes and make implicit knowledge explicit. A business analyst determines and formalizes these rules before adding data to a mini-mart. They become part of the ETL processes.

Interpretation rules are only implemented when using the data. These rules are not directly reflected in the mini-marts. Differentiating physical from interpretation rules is sometimes tricky. Watch out if data in the mini-mart has if-then-else-but transformation rules. These might hint at hidden interpretation rules like the above example of budget.

Ultimately, the data in the mini-marts has precise business meaning, scope, assumptions are made explicit, and the data is free of business interpretation.

## Conformed natural business keys

Mini-marts must be freely and easily combinable and interoperable, irrespective of their technical source or location in the data mesh. We can call this plug-and-play. We used the example of combining individual railway tracks into complex layouts to illustrate this idea. We can slightly bend an analogy from chemistry. Individual mini-marts can be combined to address specific business questions, like molecules can be synthesized from individual atoms or building blocks. Simplifying we can say that atoms share electrons to form bonds between them.

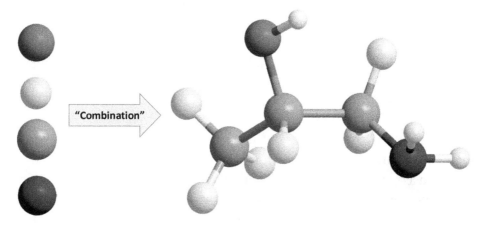

Figure 13: Assembling individual atoms into complex molecules

Mini-marts share keys to bond or connect between them. Those connections must be possible within individual mesh nodes and across mesh nodes or domains to enable data sharing and integration across the entire data mesh. This implies that mini-marts are consistent. All follow the same principles and behave the same, irrespective of where their data is sourced from or how the keys are named in the various source systems. The individual mini-marts must have consistent "keys" to be truly interoperable.

Keys based on conformed dimensions are often used to achieve this integration. "*A conformed dimension is a dimension that has the same meaning to every fact with which it relates. Conformed dimensions allow facts and measures to be categorized and described in the same way across multiple facts and/or data marts, ensuring consistent reporting across the enterprise.*"[23]

The same holds for the mini-marts. They have a set of conformed identifiers for dimensions that are consistent throughout the entire data lakehouse. Traditionally GUIDs were used for this purpose. Often GUIDs are derived via cross-referencing services.

Did you notice the words "a set of conformed identifiers" above? We shall cover those when we discuss consistent use of synonyms.

Our model enterprise has different asynchronous processes and systems. There is hardly one point in time where all data between all systems is mutually consistent and aligned. And even if such an ideal existed, it is simply not realistic to freeze processes or capture all data at that millisecond in time. In addition, there are also data errors in source systems. Consequently, we might have sales or trial data referencing customers or materials that are not yet available in the master system or are plain simple data errors. We also cannot ignore such data in our mini-marts. The creator of the respective data rightfully expects to find his data in the mini-marts, irrespective of what others think.

Traditionally, we used GUIDs to connect different data objects. Using GUIDs in the classical way creates hard dependencies between objects. All customers or materials must be available before we can process sales or trial data to look up their GUID while processing sales or trial data. Alternatively, we could create the respective entries in customer and materials while processing sales and trial data to avoid losing those entries.

The first approach forces strict sequencing of ETL processes. The latter approach results in very complex processes. Any of those would severely limit our integrated data lakehouse's extendibility, transparency, and robustness.

To circumvent these complexities, we base the connections between the mini-marts on natural business keys. This is a stark departure from traditional implementations with GUIDs—we'd never design a transactional system like this. The keys are disambiguated if needed as described further down when dwelling deeper into dimensions. This allows processing each mini-mart independently, contributing to linear versus exponential growth of complexity. The content of mini-marts is more transparent, easier to test and verify, and can cope with synonyms in a transparent way.

Any organization has ambiguities in terms. The same value might have different meanings in different "systems." Our example from above where 752445 is the customer number for Jones LLP in the transactional system used for Europe and the same number is used for Vaso Artesano

---

[23] https://www.techtarget.com/searchdatamanagement/definition/conformed-dimension.

in the system used for the Americas. We'll cover this disambiguation later when we discuss the generic data model for dimensions. Besides ambiguities, we must assume that nothing in the world has just one identifier for "one thing" or that these identifiers are unique across our enterprise's systems. In our example, both 752445 and 00x23rtA are valid customer numbers for Vaso Artesano.

Our conformed dimensions must be disambiguated to cope with ambiguities and able to inherently deal with synonyms. Ultimately, we have a defined set of dimension identifiers with aligned column naming and content standards, including synonyms and disambiguations.

# THREE

# Denormalization and Cartesian Products

This chapter covers simplifying complex application data models into easy-to-use flat tables. The data in the mini-marts, or OLAP data in general, is denormalized. This in contrast to the transactional source system's normalized entries. Denormalization makes the data much simpler to use and better suited for analysis at scale. It is done by joining source system's tables together into a simplified form, the OLAP model.

This chapter explains the various options for joining entities and looks at the risks of Cartesian products. Next we apply the same principles to JSON data structures and use classical data modeling to these structures to identify potential pitfalls.

## Denormalization

Transactional systems mostly use a highly-normalized data model. They often use what is known as the Third Normal Form (3NF). *"3NF is a database schema design approach for relational databases which uses normalizing principles to reduce the duplication of data, avoid data anomalies, ensure referential integrity, and simplify data management."*[24]

A simple example is a sales order split into a header entity and a line item entity whereby each header entity has at least one line item, and each line item belongs to precisely one header entry. Customers and order statuses are recorded at the header level, while a line item refers to each product ordered.

[24] https://en.wikipedia.org/wiki/Third_normal_form.

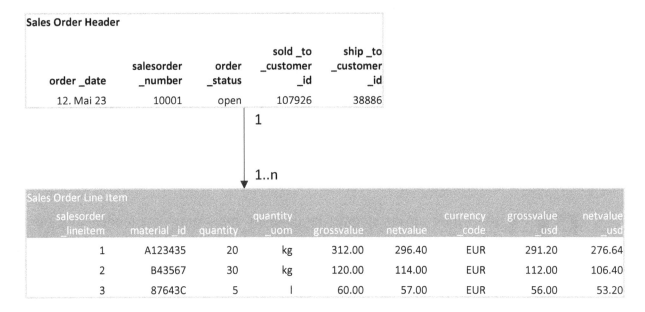

**Sales Order Header**

| order _date | salesorder _number | order _status | sold _to _customer _id | ship _to _customer _id |
|---|---|---|---|---|
| 12. Mai 23 | 10001 | open | 107926 | 38886 |

1

1..n

**Sales Order Line Item**

| salesorder _lineitem | material _id | quantity | quantity _uom | grossvalue | netvalue | currency _code | grossvalue _usd | netvalue _usd |
|---|---|---|---|---|---|---|---|---|
| 1 | A123435 | 20 | kg | 312.00 | 296.40 | EUR | 291.20 | 276.64 |
| 2 | B43567 | 30 | kg | 120.00 | 114.00 | EUR | 112.00 | 106.40 |
| 3 | 87643C | 5 | l | 60.00 | 57.00 | EUR | 56.00 | 53.20 |

Figure 14: Basic entity relationship example[25]

Querying such data requires joining headers and line items. While this is simple for one type of object and source, the application's data model needs to be understood. Moreover, it grows increasingly complex as the data models become more complex as multiple source systems consolidate into one mini-mart, and the data generalizes to make querying easier.

The AfterAcademy learning platform states it well: *"Denormalization is a database optimization technique where we add redundant data in the database to get rid of the complex join operations. This is done to speed up database access speed. Denormalization is done after normalization for improving the performance of the database. The data from one table is included in another table to reduce the number of joins in the query and hence helps in speeding up the performance."* [26]

Simply put, denormalization combines what previously were multiple small tables into one larger, flatter, and broader table, reducing the need to join data for querying.

| order _date | salesorder _number | order _status | sold _to _customer _id | ship _to _customer _id | salesorder _lineitem | material _id | quantity | quantity _uom | grossvalue | netvalue | currency _code | grossvalue _usd | netvalue _usd |
|---|---|---|---|---|---|---|---|---|---|---|---|---|---|
| 12. Mai 23 | 10001 | open | 107926 | 38886 | 1 | A123435 | 20 | kg | 312.00 | 296.40 | EUR | 291.20 | 276.64 |
| 12. Mai 23 | 10001 | open | 107926 | 38886 | 2 | B43567 | 30 | kg | 120.00 | 114.00 | EUR | 112.00 | 106.40 |
| 12. Mai 23 | 10001 | open | 107926 | 38886 | 3 | 87643C | 5 | l | 60.00 | 57.00 | EUR | 56.00 | 53.20 |

Figure 15: Data join result

---

[25] This book mostly uses "." as decimal point and " ' " for digit grouping. This as a concession to the different local conventions across the globe that is not misleading either, see
https://en.wikipedia.org/wiki/Decimal_separator#Digit_grouping.

[26] https://afteracademy.com/blog/what-is-denormalization-in-dbms.

# Attribute categories

We can put every attribute or column into one of three categories. These categories later define the finer rules for denormalizing the data while guaranteeing correct query results by default.

- **Business key**. This term refers to columns that form the unique business key, the identifier by which the user frequently refers to individual data. In the above example, salesorder_number and salesorder_lineitem are such business keys. These business keys might require disambiguation if data is generalized from different sources and subtypes into the same mini-mart.

- **Dimensions and classifying columns**. Dimension columns join with our dimensions, while classifying columns don't necessarily refer to formal dimensions; they contextualize an entry. Sold_to- and ship_to_customer and material_id, currency, and quantity_uom are dimensions while order_date, order_status, order_type, or record_type where applicable, are classifying attributes. They further qualify for entry. Dimensions and classifying attributes can repeat during denormalization without the risk of falsifying results.

- **Measures**. Wikipedia defines measure as *"a property on which calculations [e.g., sum, count, average, minimum, maximum] can be made."*[27] I describe measures colloquially as the "payload" of facts. Repeating measures in a denormalized table leads to erroneous results. This is the essential reason for multi-layered facts and other techniques to avoid Cartesian products, as we will see later.

In this chapter, we will develop an essential awareness of the risks of Cartesian products that will drive some of the design decisions we will be making.

Let's look at a simple relational model, an extension of the above example. Here, we have a prepayment under the sales order header. Prepayment is a measure. We also have measures on the line item, showing each product's value. We can see in the example prepayment that the total prepayment is $410, while the full value of the products is $1,160.

---

[27] https://en.wikipedia.org/wiki/Measure_(data_warehouse).

# Cartesian products

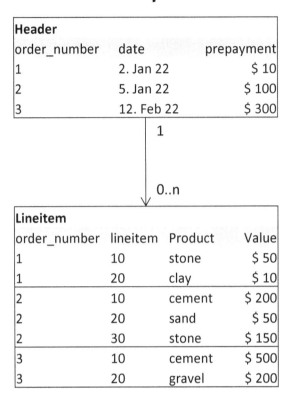

Figure 16: ER model example with measures at different granularities

Now we join the data based on the order_number.

```
1    select
2         h.*
3         ,l.lineitem , l.product, l.value
4      from header   h
5      join lineitem l on h.order_number = l.order_number
```

Sample Code 1: Simple join

Joined

| order_number | date | prepayment | lineitem | Product | Value |
|---|---|---|---|---|---|
| 1 | 2. Jan. 22 | $10 | 10 | stone | $50 |
| 1 | 2.Jan. 22 | $10 | 20 | clay | $10 |
| 2 | 5. Jan. 22 | $100 | 10 | cement | $200 |
| 2 | 5. Jan. 22 | $100 | 20 | sand | $50 |
| 2 | 5. Jan. 22 | $100 | 30 | stone | $150 |
| 3 | 12. Feb. 22 | $300 | 10 | cement | $500 |
| 3 | 12. Feb. 22 | $300 | 20 | gravel | $200 |
| | | $920 | | | $1,160 |

Figure 17: Sample join leading to erroneous sum

The total prepayment suddenly more than doubles from $410 to $920. This is due to the Cartesian product on order_number. Each header line repeats as often as there are line items. Of course, this is not acceptable as it will lead to incorrect numbers on reports.

A user can take special precautions when reading the data. For example, she might calculate the sums for prepayment and for the total product value separately, calculating the sum of the prepayments based on the distinct prepayment values for each distinct order_number. A user must know the precise data model. We will see in the chapter about multi-layered facts that there is a better option to avoid the pitfalls of the Cartesian product. It will allow a user to query the data and get correct values without special precautions.

## Erroneous data

The above data model explains the theory. An enterprise data lakehouse deals with actual data. Actual data tends to be erroneous in places, mainly if millions or billions of records exist.

Let's look at potential erroneous data and what it means for querying. There might be two entries in the header for the same order_number. There might be entries in the line item for an order number that does not appear in the header. This accurate data contradicts the theoretical data model. In reality, there is a many-to-many relationship between headers and line items. This results in erroneous values.

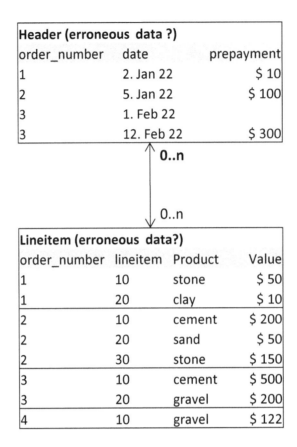

Figure 18: ER model of erroneous data

The total prepayment is still $410, while the full value of the products is $1,282. This includes the additional $122 for gravel with order_number 4.

Let's join these two entities to account for missing header entries. Notice that we do a right outer join, selecting all values for line items and the matching header records.

```
select
        h.*
        ,l.lineitem , l.product, l.value
    from header h
    right join lineitem l on h.order_number = l.order_number
```

Sample Code 2: Outer join for erroneous data

| order_number | date | prepayment | lineitem | Product | Value |
|---|---|---|---|---|---|
| 1 | 2. Jan. 22 | $10 | 10 | stone | $50 |
| 1 | 2. Jan. 22 | $10 | 20 | clay | $10 |
| 2 | 5. Jan. 22 | $100 | 10 | cement | $200 |
| 2 | 5. Jan. 22 | $100 | 20 | sand | $50 |
| 2 | 5. Jan. 22 | $100 | 30 | stone | $150 |
| 3 | 1. Feb. 22 | | 10 | cement | $500 |
| 3 | 1. Feb. 22 | | 20 | gravel | $200 |
| 3 | 12. Feb. 22 | $300 | 10 | cement | $500 |
| 3 | 12. Feb. 22 | $300 | 20 | gravel | $200 |
| 4 | | | 10 | gravel | $122 |
| | | $920 | | | $1,982 |

Figure 19: Sample erroneous data

The total prepayment is still $920, the same erroneous value from our earlier query. The total value of the products increased from $1,282 to the erroneous $1,982. This is because we have two entries in the header for order_number 3.

Our enterprise data lakehouse must be robust about such errors and process them in a predefined way. Verify the theoretical data model with check queries to ensure the practice matches the theory or to account for erroneous data when preparing the data marts. Error handling depends on the outcome of the business analysis. Always assume the worst and make the processes as robust as possible. We will see further along in the ETL processes how we can account for those pitfalls when preparing our data marts. This keeps users from falling into the same trap and reporting inflated sales values.

## JSON data and data models

We used a simple Entity Relationship (ER) model above to explain the data and the source of errors. The data model was very explicit in the above example. Any JSON data has an embedded data model. We risk the same pitfalls and mistakes when processing JSON data, and we can use the same techniques to prevent them.

Let's take a JSON example, translate it into an ER model, and then analyze its specifics. We use an example of a recipe whereby each component can be one of the multiple options, such as, "We can use stone or gravel." In the JSON, this is an array of optional products within each line item.

We see that each array in the JSON translates into a one-to-many relationship in the ER model.

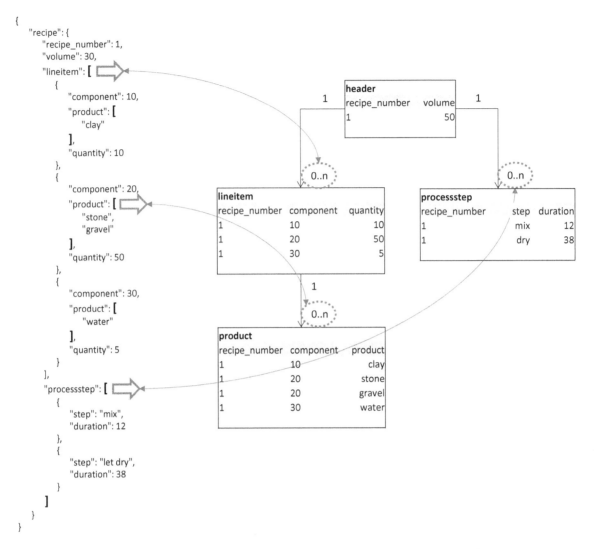

```
{
  "recipe": {
    "recipe_number": 1,
    "volume": 30,
    "lineitem": [
      {
        "component": 10,
        "product": [
          "clay"
        ],
        "quantity": 10
      },
      {
        "component": 20,
        "product": [
          "stone",
          "gravel"
        ],
        "quantity": 50
      },
      {
        "component": 30,
        "product": [
          "water"
        ],
        "quantity": 5
      }
    ],
    "processstep": [
      {
        "step": "mix",
        "duration": 12
      },
      {
        "step": "let dry",
        "duration": 38
      }
    ]
  }
}
```

Figure 20: Mapping a recipe JSON with options onto an ER model

```
1   select
2           h.recipe_number , h.volume
3           ,l.component, l.quantity
4           ,p.product
5           ,s.step   , s.duration
6       from header       h
7       join lineitem     l on h.recipe_number = l.recipe_number
8       join product      p on l.recipe_number = p.recipe_number
                              and l.component = p.component
9       join processstep s on h.recipe_number = s.recipe_number
        order by 1,3 ;
```

Sample Code 3: Sample join for illustration of the recipe with options

The previous example explained what happens if we combine data from a one-to-many relationship. The result is a compounded Cartesian product.

| recipe _number | volume | component | quantity | product | step | duration |
|---|---|---|---|---|---|---|
| 1 | 50 | 10 | 10 | clay | dry | 38 |
| 1 | 50 | 10 | 10 | clay | mix | 12 |
| 1 | 50 | 20 | 50 | gravel | dry | 38 |
| 1 | 50 | 20 | 50 | stone | dry | 38 |
| 1 | 50 | 20 | 50 | gravel | mix | 12 |
| 1 | 50 | 20 | 50 | stone | mix | 12 |
| 1 | 50 | 30 | 5 | water | dry | 38 |
| 1 | 50 | 30 | 5 | water | mix | 12 |
| | 400 | | 230 | | | 200 |

Figure 21: Sample data with cartesian products from a default join for a recipe with options

Such a mini-mart would return an incorrect sum of values. Of course, we can do similar manipulations as outlined above to get the correct value. If we know that quantity is per component, we can run a subselect listing the specific amounts per component and then join this with other data. If we learn that durations are for all the steps within the recipe, then we can run a subselect for those as well. Then we join these to get our correct totals. But this is cumbersome. Those manipulations require intrinsic knowledge of the source data model. We do not want to burden the user of the data marts with the complexities of untangling all of the above again.

Knowing hidden cardinalities in JSON structures and how they translate any JSON into the corresponding ER model. In the chapter on multi-layered facts, how to convert the same data into a fact table that always returns the correct data and totals.

# FOUR

# Design Blueprint Overview

In this chapter, we introduce the two distinct design blueprints of mini-marts and then explore them in detail in subsequent chapters.

## Conventions

Colloquially, we can say that facts capture measures or "transactional data," while dimensions capture reference information.

Dimensions, or more precisely the identifiers for those, follow strict naming conventions. This is essential for making the mini-marts and the connections between them usable and understandable for any user. If it is a customer_id, the column name in facts can be ship_to_customer_id or complaint_customer_id. Both refer to the Customer dimension. Likewise, material_id, finished_material_id, and component_material_id refer to the same dimension multiple times. The respective column names are closely monitored, strictly defined, and apply similarly across all mini-marts in our enterprise lakehouse.

We use simplified examples to illustrate some of the concepts. These examples blend concepts with techniques and models from actual use. Terms like "customer" and "sales order" are proxies to illustrate concepts. They are then translated into examples using *mm01_customer* or *mm20_sales_order* as physical entities for our mini-marts. These prefixes and unique numbers for mini-marts [like mm01_] are very helpful in a real-world implementation. Furthermore, we use the convention of *mm<nn>_t_<descriptor>*, for example, *mm01_t_customer_main*, to differentiate tables from views like *mm01_customer_main*. (Data consumers must never access the tables directly—more on this later.)

We discussed the independence and modularity of the mini-marts and conformed natural business keys. For these reasons, GUIDs are never used between mini-marts or to link facts with dimensions. GUIDs are only valid and meaningful within mini-marts. Relations between mini-marts are based on natural business keys.

Generalization can lead to sparsely populated tables, while denormalization, historicization, or version control leads to repeated values. Content in columns reflects "things we know about a thing." An empty range indicates we do not know a "certain thing." Data quality rules indicate what we should know about a "thing." Yet we might know more or less for any of the generalized objects irrespective of the subtype of an object.

Repeated values are a consequence of denormalization and historicization. Sometimes the term "slowly changing dimension" is used. I am not fond of this term. What is the boundary between "slowly changing" and "fast-changing"? Either an object must be version controlled, keeping track of content changes, or not. We will introduce a generic concept for historicization. If a mini-mart must keep track of changes, then the mini-mart is of type 2. This is irrespective of whether it is a fact or a dimension, slow or fast changing.

As stated, modern technologies make such generic designs possible and mitigate the consequences.

## Overview

Each mini-mart is a small set of physical tables, often just one. We build the entire enterprise data lakehouse using only two different design blueprints. Here we introduce them and then describe them in more detail in future chapters. They are designed so that they effortlessly combine together and can account for the pitfalls described above. Specifically:

- Facts are highly denormalized objects and capture measures and other things. Facts are the result of transactions or measurements. Facts are often, but not always, sets of quantitative measures. Facts in our mini-marts can be structured within themselves, more in multi-layer facts.

- Dimensions are reference information. Dimensions in our enterprise data lakehouse always have synonyms, can have relationships between different entries in dimensions and can have flexible lists of additional properties.

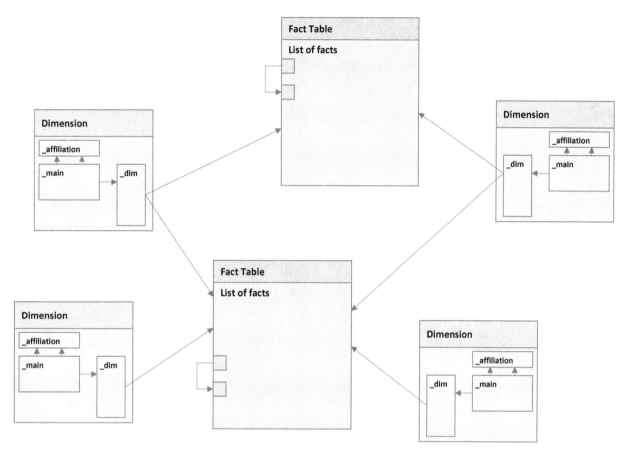

Figure 22: Snowflake models from mini-marts

These dimensions and facts are combined to address a specific business question, as outlined in the example about weather, sales, and trials in the introduction.

The connections between the mini-marts are based on common dimensions and reserved IDs. Common dimensions are sometimes called conformed dimensions. They have a consistent meaning throughout the entire data lakehouse. The IDs are natural business keys, such as business_partner_id and material_id. This is a stark departure from traditional implementations. Using natural business keys instead of GUIDs to relate data across multiple mini-marts allows for parallel, asynchronous ETL processes in heterogenous systems in our model enterprise and asynchronous data quality processes. The finer aspects, such as the disambiguation of those keys, are covered later.

One dimension can appear multiple times in the fact table such as sold-to_customer_id and ship-to_customer_id. Both refer to the Customer dimension. The same applies to material_ids, where finished_material_id and component_material_id refer multiple times to the same dimension.

# FIVE

# Facts

This chapter deals with HOW MUCH—long lists of facts, numbers, and measures that are sometimes even at different granularities.

## Introduction to facts

This chapter explains various aspects of fact tables. A similar chapter about dimensions follows.

Facts are the hub(s) in the snowflake or star model. Roughly stated, facts are long lists with measures, classifying columns, and references to dimensions. Facts are denormalized for easy consumption. The facts for an enterprise data lakehouse are no different, with a few additional features:

- They are always at the finest grain

- They are generalized and can consolidate data from various source systems

- They contain disambiguated natural business keys to dimensions

- They can have a nested structure within themselves, which will result in multi-layer facts

- They can normalize roles for customers/business partners, such as in PartnerReference

We will focus on facts here and on dimensions later.

We use Sales Orders as an example for illustration purposes, but the concepts apply to any other object. Other objects could be delivery, marketing plan, trial, process order, invoice, bill of materials, web traffic, etc. In the denormalization chapter, we examined a sales order reflected in most transactional systems in 3NF as a header-table and a line-item table, often containing further detailed information and tables. The same data is denormalized in our mini-mart, where header columns are repeated as often as there are line-items. This simplifies the use of the data, allows for great flexibility for consolidating data from multiple source systems, and avoids always having to join them explicitly, which speeds things up.

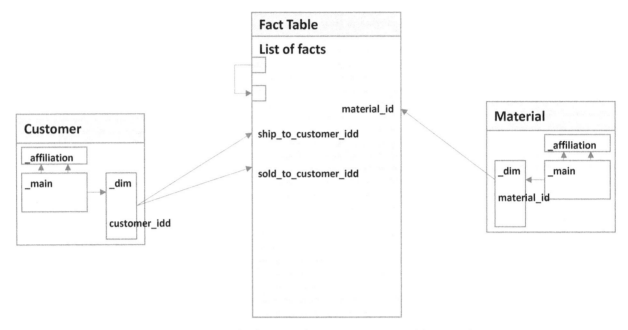

Figure 23: Facts and relation to dimensions via natural business keys

With some exceptions, as explained below, facts look very similar to the data we had previously when we reviewed denormalization and joined a sales order header with its line items.

| order _date | salesorder _number | order _status | sold _to _customer _id | ship _to _customer _id | salesorder lineitem | material _id | quantity | quantity _uom | grossvalue | netvalue | currency code | grossvalue usd | netvalue usd |
|---|---|---|---|---|---|---|---|---|---|---|---|---|---|
| 12. Mai 23 | 10001 | open | 107926 | 38886 | 1 | A123435 | 20 | kg | 312.00 | 296.40 | EUR | 291.20 | 276.64 |
| 12. Mai 23 | 10001 | open | 107926 | 38886 | 2 | B43567 | 30 | kg | 120.00 | 114.00 | EUR | 112.00 | 106.40 |
| 12. Mai 23 | 10001 | open | 107926 | 38886 | 3 | 87643C | 5 | l | 60.00 | 57.00 | EUR | 56.00 | 53.20 |

Figure 24: Result of data joining, a simple fact table

This is a simple fact table, a simple join between a header and a line item table. It contains dimensions and classifying columns from both, but the measures such as quantity, gross and net values are for individual line items only. They do not contain customer names or material descriptions but rather the customer_id and the material_id. The respective descriptions are then with the dimensions themselves.

## Granularity and derived values

Watch out for facts at mixed granularity or derived facts that are actually a combination of facts from multiple mini-marts. Facts capture the measures at the finest granularity where it is available. A typical example is quantities of sales order line items and not of sales order header. Later, we will look at multi-layer facts, which can be at different cardinalities.

Even a simple sales order fact usually has many columns, such as different currency values, blocking status, etc. I have seen an implementation in which a Sales Order has 590 columns. This ought to be an exception. In our example, all columns are inherent to a sales order or line item. We store these in the facts mini-mart for sales orders. Any fact is stored in the mini-marts at the finest grain. KPIs can be stored with the sales order facts if they are inherently based on the lowest grain of sales order. Some of them can contribute to derived KPIs at the same granularity. One example can be quantity_not_confirmed, assuming a sales order has quantity ordered and quantity confirmed.

There are often additional derived values or KPIs that combine facts from multiple mini-marts, such as orders not yet delivered, orders not yet invoiced, or charges not yet paid. Those combine data from sales orders with data from deliveries or invoices. The latter two differ in granularity to sales orders, making integration difficult. A sales order might be split into multiple deliveries or invoiced in various installments. All of them are individual fact mini-marts with different granularities. You will have a mini-mart for sales orders, one for delivery, and one for invoices. Any sales order can refer to any number of deliveries and invoices. Likewise, a delivery can consist of several combined sales orders. But we would want to know the quantities of sales order line items not yet delivered.

This is a cross-mart KPI. It combines data from sales orders and deliveries. Yet we cannot simply join those together for the reasons outlined in the chapter on Cartesian products. We would inflate the sales quantity if we had multiple deliveries. We can correctly calculate the amounts not yet delivered only if we summarize all deliveries for a specific line item first and then compare this sum with the ordered quantities. Such cross-mart KPIs require aggregating one mini-mart data to match it to the granularity of another mini-mart.

Derived KPIs must be readily available when creating any analysis. There are two options for handling these derived KPIs: making them part of the same mini-mart or deriving them at reporting time.

The first option calculates these cross-mart KPIs during ETL for the mini-mart mostly while processing sales_order but updates them on any change in dependent objects like deliveries or invoices. This approach requires updating a mini-mart upon changes to another mini-mart, resulting in quite complex and entangled ETL processes. It can be error-prone and difficult to reconcile. It is more transparent to create separate mini-marts, one each for sales_order, delivery, and invoice, each at its finest granularity. Derived key figures are then calculated by combining the individual basic mini-marts in views or materialized views. The result is timelier and reflects the actual stage at that specific moment without relying on nested ETL processes. The approach is outlined in more detail in the chapter about usage simplifications. This will become a KPI-view.

# Business key proxy

This chapter examines flexibility for unique business keys from different source systems while keeping ETL processes lean and mean. It will later become relevant for the ETL processes but also below when we look at multi-layer facts.

One additional yet important concept is added to the facts: the GUIDs. Yes, there are GUIDs, despite what was said before. But these GUIDs are only valid and applicable within a mini-mart, never to join different mini-marts together. The GUIDs are derived from the unique business keys. The business keys from each contributing source system don't have to be identical. GUIDs serve a few purposes:

- Consolidate and generalize data from multiple sources into the same mini-mart. These sources and subtypes might not have the same columns as unique business keys. The fact_guid is a technical proxy for a unique business key irrespective of source system or object type. It has no other meaning.

- Expedite data load while preventing duplicated data.

- They can reflect the relationship of facts at different granularity within the same mini-mart. You might recall the example where prepayment is at the order level, product quantities are at the line item or the example of total committed value for a sales plan versus individual product quantities at the item level. Those will result in Multi-Layer Facts.

Here we have now added the fact_guid.[28]

| fact_guid | order_date | salesorder _number | salesorder _lineitem | order _status | source _system _cde | sold_to _customer_id | ship_to _customer_id | material_id | quantity | quantity _uom |
|---|---|---|---|---|---|---|---|---|---|---|
| f1dd7064 | 12. May 23 | 10001 | 1 | open | sapab | 107926 | 825456 | A123435 | 20 | kg |
| de1c1a18 | 12. May 23 | 10001 | 2 | open | sapab | 107926 | 825456 | B43567 | 30 | kg |
| 9a58545e | 12. May 23 | 10001 | 3 | open | sapab | 107926 | 825456 | 87643C | 5 | l |
| : | : | : | : | : | : | : | : | : | : | : |

Figure 25: Sample sales order data

---

[28] GUIDs are shorted for readability.

```
fact_guid = md5(salesorder_number || salesorder_itemnumber || source_system_cde)
```

Sample Code 4: Sample calculation of fact_guid

In the above example, fact_guid is derived from sales order number, line item, and source system. This embeds knowledge about the source system coined into the mini-marts ETL process. Fact_guid will later be used to facilitate generic upserts of the mini-marts.

---

# Multi-layer facts

In this chapter, we look at the correct analysis of facts at different granularity, avoiding erroneous Cartesian products.

Preamble: "Multi-layer facts" should NOT be confused with "infinite hierarchies." Multi-layer facts are not hierarchies. Multi-layer facts are strictly for situations where the finest grain sources inherently have measures at different granularity within the same business object. Classical flexible hierarchies are addressed through _affiliation and _ladder in dimensions.

You might have noticed the little caveat in the Granularity and Derived Values sentence: "*KPIs can be stored with the sales order facts if they are inherently based on the lowest grain of sales order. In our simplified example, this is the sales order line item.*" What if they are not at the exact same grain? What if there is a net price for each line item, but the total order value is not the sum of the line items due to the overall discounts given? Multi-layer facts account for such data in a way that makes using the data easy. This is not the same as a sales order that has multiple deliveries. Deliveries might contain items from multiple sales orders and large orders sent in multiple shipments, while they all might appear in a single invoice. To address these, we affiliate facts with each other (see the chapter on fact affiliation). Multi-layer facts apply strictly within one atomic mini-mart.

Before going into detail, let's quickly assess alternatives. We can store data in its original 3NF tables and have joins. Combining such data might lead to Cartesian products, as described in the Denormalization and Cartesian Products chapter. It will be challenging to create views that do not erroneously inflate measures. This can be done with union views, but they will ultimately look like multi-layer facts. The complexities are compounded if data from different sources is consolidated into the same mini-mart to create a truly-integrated enterprise data lakehouse.

We avoid the pitfalls of Cartesian products by implementing mini-marts containing data at different granularity as multi-layer facts. It offers greater resilience and flexibility. Multi-layer fact tables are easy to extend and consolidate data from various sources.

The design of multi-layer facts is best illustrated in an example. We have seen the perils of Cartesian products in our discussion of joins and the hidden cardinalities of JSON structures.

We will use a sales plan example to illustrate multi-layer facts, as it more readily shows the relationships with dimensions. It has the same principles and risks of Cartesian products that we have seen before. A sales plan's committed value might be different from the total of the planned values per product.

We have two entities and each has at least one measure: the committed value for a sales plan and the planned quantities and values for individual products. These two measures are at different granularity. They are at the header versus line item level.

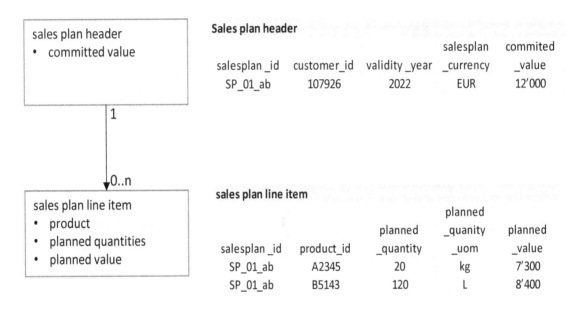

Figure 26: Example salesplan ER model

Simply joining the two entities together on salesplan_id yields the data below.

Incorrect example............................

| fact_guid | source _system _cde | salesplan_id | customer_id | validity _year | salesplan _currency | commited _value | product_id | planned _quantity | planned _quanity _uom | planned _value |
|---|---|---|---|---|---|---|---|---|---|---|
| 879a58545e2a | sfdc | SP_01_ab | 107926 | 2022 | EUR | 12'000 | A2345 | 20 | kg | 7'300 |
| b12d20b8b9cc | sfdc | SP_01_ab | 107926 | 2022 | EUR | 12'000 | B5143 | 120 | L | 8'400 |

Figure 27: Sample data for a simple join for salesplan

The result of querying the sum of committed_values across all sales plans for a given year will be $24,000, twice the amount. Getting the correct result requires special precautions and knowledge of the internal structure of sales plans. The respective query can be very tricky. In essence, it requires knowing that salesplan_id is the unique key. She can then do the same tricks explained in Cartesian Products, this time calculating the sum of the committed values based on the distinct values for each specific sales plan and joining this with the sum of the planned values if needed.

```
1  Select salesplan_id,
2      max(committed_value)  as committed_value
3      from mm05_salesplan
4      group by salesplan_id
5      ;
```

Sample Code 5: An awkward way to retrieve the committed value for a sales plan

This is not ideal and has a significant risk of reporting incorrect data.[29] We use multi-layer facts to make use of such data easier.

- Queries must be simple and not require special business knowledge beyond the documentation about how GUIDs are related. A consumer should not take special precautions to get the correct totals of committed values.

- Any combination of columns can easily filter any data without knowing the source object's internal structures.

- No measure is duplicated. A query on any measure always returns the correct values, irrespective of where this measure is present.

There are several ways of counteracting the above challenge. They all pose their drawbacks. The approach presented here favors the ability to easily consolidate and query data from various sources for the price of needing a columnar store to handle repeated values efficiently. The above Salesplan data as multi-layer facts result in the following fact table.[30]

| l0_guid | l1_guid | fact_guid | record_type | mm_record_level | source_system_cde | salesplan_id | customer_id | validity_year | salesplan_currency | committed_value | product_id | planned_value | planned_quantity | planned_quanity_uom |
|---|---|---|---|---|---|---|---|---|---|---|---|---|---|---|
| 1dd70 | | 1dd70 | header | 0 | sfdc | SP_01_ab | 0bf478c391f9 | 2023 | EUR | 12'000 | | | | |
| 1dd70 | 879a5 | 879a5 | lineitem | 1 | sfdc | SP_01_ab | 0bf478c391f9 | 2023 | EUR | | A2345 | 7'300 | 20 | kg |
| 1dd70 | b12d2 | b12d2 | lineitem | 1 | sfdc | SP_01_ab | 0bf478c391f9 | 2023 | EUR | | B5143 | 8'400 | 120 | L |

Figure 28: Example of multi-layer facts for salesplan

---

[29] It might be tempting to go back to the original 3NF of the transactional system. This forgoes all benefits of an OLAP model and impacts the ability to integrate data from multiple sources. Using the multi-layer approach is more robust and easier, although it requires more engineering for the ETL processes.

[30] The GUIDs are shorted to increase readability.

Multi-layer facts follow a set of rules.

1.  Each record is qualified with a record_type, such as a header and a line item in the above example, and has a specific record_level.

2.  All line items belonging to the same Salesplan header share the same l0_guid. This relationship is critical for advanced queries. The number of levels [L0, L1, L2_GUID] corresponds to the different granularities of the source system. The lowest level GUID and fact_guid are almost redundant. Both are kept in the mini-mart to ensure consistency in naming and avoid yes-but explanations.

3.  Classifying columns and dimensions such as customer_id or validity_year are repeated on all record_types to which they apply. We can query any line item on its header's properties without even knowing the internal structure. This meets the second bullet point above.

4.  Measures are only present at the granularity where they apply. In the example, committed values are current at the header record, while planned_value is only at the item level. This satisfies the third bullet above on having no duplicate measures.

We can easily query and aggregate any measure, leading to the correct result and never resulting in a Cartesian product. For example:

**select sum**(*committed_value*) ***from*** ... ***where*** *validity_year = 2023*
**select sum**(*planned_value*) ***from*** ... ***where*** *validity_year = 2023.*

Here we return the correct values, with no risk of Cartesian products for any measure. Even **select sum**(committed_value)- **sum**(planned_value) **from** ... **where** validity_year = 2023 and any combination and aggregation thereof return correct values efficiently and without any particular precaution for the internal structure of the sales plan.

Avoiding Cartesian products results in slightly higher complexity when filtering for measures at different granularities. These require a self-join of entries on L0_guid. In other words, this means "return all line items whose header has a committed value above 10,000." The sentence "line items whose header" indicates the self-join.

The naming L0_guid, L1_guid, etc., evolved after some learning. In one of our first implementations, we used GUIDs named for context, such as *process_guid* or *assessment_guid*. Using them requires context knowledge to transpose the data for the data science feature derivation. It is also complicated as additional sources get added to the same mini-mart with slightly different contexts. The generic naming (L0, L1) and an explicit *mm_record_level* and *record_type*, helps mitigate those drawbacks and scales better.

Mitigating faulty Cartesian products in "normal join" is substantially more complex than self-joins if measures at different granularities must be filtered and combined. Multi-layer facts inherently eliminate the risk of reporting inflated numbers.

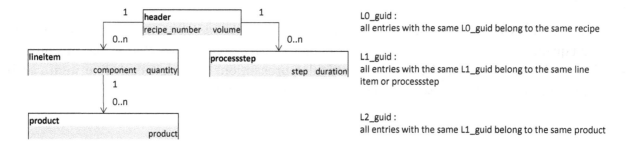

Figure 29: Model of more than one dependent segment or child object

Sales Order and Salesplan were simple examples. There are situations like our JSON example with alternate products. These are more complex but, again, can be addressed from our mini-mart. Fact table in the above example:

| l0_guid | l1_guid | l2_guid | mm_record _level | record_typ e | fact_guid | Recipe _number | volume | component | quantity | product | step | duration |
|---|---|---|---|---|---|---|---|---|---|---|---|---|
| ca423 | | | 0 | header | ca423 | 1 | 50 | | | | | |
| ca423 | 93f98 | | 1 | lineitem | 93f98 | 1 | | 10 | 10 | | | |
| ca423 | 93f98 | 7e6c0 | 2 | product | 7e6c0 | 1 | | 10 | | clay | | |
| ca423 | 86192 | | 1 | lineitem | 86192 | 1 | | 30 | 5 | | | |
| ca423 | 86192 | f28bc | 2 | product | f28bc | 1 | | 30 | | water | | |
| ca423 | 4fb5c | | 1 | lineitem | 4fb5c | 1 | | 20 | 50 | | | |
| ca423 | 4fb5c | c8a2f | 2 | product | c8a2f | 1 | | 20 | | gravel | | |
| ca423 | 4fb5c | 4dc74 | 2 | product | 4dc74 | 1 | | 20 | | stone | | |
| ca423 | ce7d1 | | 1 | processstep | ce7d1 | 1 | | | | | mix | 12 |
| ca423 | 93cd6 | | 1 | processstep | 93cd6 | 1 | | | | | dry | 38 |

Figure 30: Sample multi-layer facts for multiple segments

We can see that products and quantities are different record_types. This is different than in our sales order example. In a sales order, each line item has precisely one material and its quantity; the quantity is at the same granularity as the material. Such data is much simpler. In the recipe example, any component can be one or multiple materials but only one quantity.

There can be many different questions/queries for the above situation. A simple example is: List all quantities and the list of products I can use for each component. Notice that this query is in strict business terms. We take no particular precaution. Although each line item can have multiple alternate materials, the measures returned are correct.

```
1    select
2            recipe_number
3            ,component
4            ,sum(quantity) as quantity
5            ,listagg(product, ' or ')  as list_of_products
6        from mm02_recipe_fact
7        group by 1,2
8        order by 1,2
```

Sample Code 6: Multi-layer facts example listing alternate products

| recipe_number | component | quantity | list_of_products |
|---|---|---|---|
| 1 | 10 | 10 | clay |
| 1 | 20 | 50 | stone or gravel |
| 1 | 30 | 5 | water |

Figure 31: Sample list with alternate products

We can achieve the same results by simply listing and not summing up the quantity. This is correct in the unique situation where the amount coincidentally is at the same granularity as the sum the query asks for. Making the usage rules for a mini-mart dependent on coincidence is not recommended. Using multi-layer facts returns correct values irrespective of coincidence. We can calculate the sum of any measures across any filters without the risk of inflated measures. The following result uses traditional joins across the header, line item, and product, and contrasts with the example.

| recipe_number | resulting_volume | total_input_quantities | list_of_products |
|---|---|---|---|
| 1 | 50 | 65 | clay , stone , gravel , drinking water |

Figure 32: Sample output of aggregation using multi-layer facts

```
1 select  recipe_number
2         ,sum(volume)              as resulting_volume
3         ,sum(quantity)            as total_input_quantity
4         ,listagg(product, ' , ')  as list_of_products
5     from mm02_t_recipe_fact
6     group by 1 order by 1
```

Sample Code 7: Robust aggregations using multi-layer facts

# Partner_reference in facts

This is a case of relating facts with dimensions, giving great flexibility. In this chapter, we look at 360° customer views. We address flexibility in customer analysis across a customer's roles in different processes.

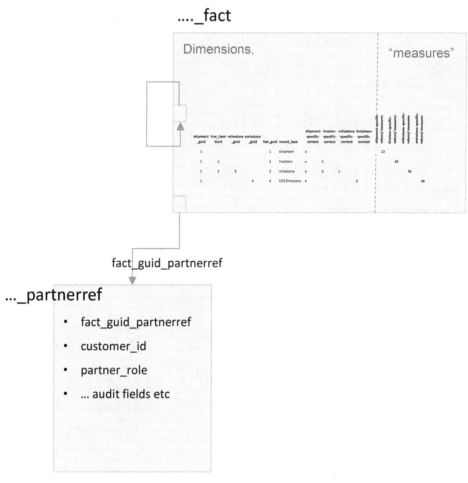

Figure 33: Facts with partner reference

The simple example of sales_order we had initially has only two customer roles, sold_to and ship_to. This is a gross simplification. There are many more customer roles, even in a simple fact like sales order. It gets increasingly complex as different processes target different customer roles.

We originally developed the generic partner reference concept to adjust elegantly and flexibly to different go-to-market strategies and sales plan processes, yet the concept is generic. One country's go-to-market system might focus on ship-to customers, while another focuses its sales plans on sold-to customers and marketing activities on payers. We can handle all those roles with different customer columns in our fact table. Depending on a country's specific process, this will lead to various query statements. It requires adapting those queries to different business questions and combinations of facts.

It is more elegant and flexible to make these adaptations dynamically. We use an auxiliary table to facts called partner reference [_partnerref]. _partnerref contains the list of customers (partners) and their roles for each record in our facts. Joining the customer dimension [customer_id] is not done through the customer_id column in the _fact table but through _partnerref, varying the partner role. Analysis and insight gains across different and even multiple customer roles are more agile and dynamic, especially across different roles of the same customer in other processes.

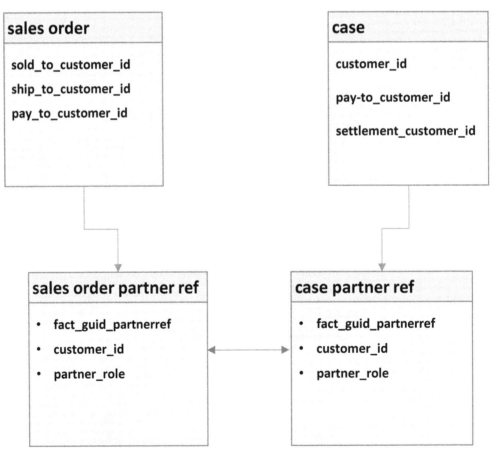

Figure 34: Dynamically combing data across different partner roles

Our enterprise mart has become more flexible, adjusting to the different go-to-market strategies, while data analysis is more agile and dynamic, needing fewer changes to adapt.

```
1 select sf.*, cf.*
2     from mm03_salesorder_fact          sf
3     join mm03_salesorder_partner_ref   sp  on sf.fact_guid   = sp.fact_guid
4     join mm07_case_partner_ref         cp  on sp.customer_id = cp.customer_id
5     join mm07_case_fact                cf  on cf.fact_guid   = cp.fact_guid
6     where sp.partner_role = 'sold-to'
7       and cp.partner_role = 'settlement'
8     ;
```

Sample Code 8: Using partner_ref for dynamic joins

Note that in lines 6 and 7, we can select the respective partner roles, even as parameters, without needing to change the query statement itself.

Not using partner_ref requires hardcoding the roles into the query between sales order and case. Partner_ref allows the analyst to add a dedicated parameter into the where clause, as lines 6 and 7 in the above example. He can dynamically alter this clause and immediately assess the outcome. In the above example, the analyst can flexibly filter for different combinations of roles of sales order and cases on which the data is compared. This reduces the number of queries that must be maintained, reducing costs and increasing flexibility. The partner role is explicitly made visible, which is another advantage. It avoids guessing which partner roles are being combined in the query.

---

## Facts affiliations

In this chapter, we look at many-to-many relationships between facts. We will see a similar concept later when we look at affiliations[31] within dimensions. The chapter about affiliation in dimensions shows how affiliations enable dynamic, flexible, unbalanced hierarchies between entries within the same mini-mart.

The current chapter describes affiliations between fact mini-marts. Let's assume a sales order has multiple deliveries, deliveries can be sent in multiple shipments. For example, imagine multiple shipments created for a delivery item where the quantity is enormous, exceeding the capacity of a single truck or a 40-foot container. In contrast, all orders might be consolidated in one invoice only.

---

[31] The term "affiliation" is used consistently for the concept and the physical implementation.

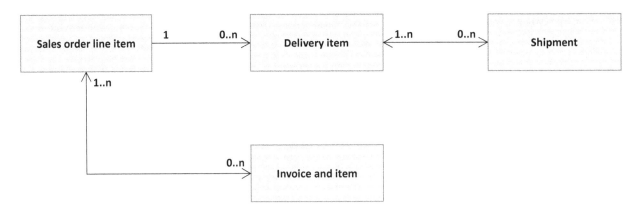

Figure 35: Example of relationships between transactional objects

The example is a bit overstated in places to make a point on a complex situation. I will take this opportunity to introduce another aspect of generalization, which is a generalization concerning cardinalities: "One is a subset of many." In other words, if a solution can handle many entries, it can also take single entries. Let's illustrate it in the above example. There might be only a few deliveries or delivery line items split into multiple shipments. Some source systems might even have the shipment information directly at the delivery point while you receive detailed shipment information now from the logistics company. This detailed information has consolidated shipments, containers containing items from multiple deliveries, and loads for the same delivery line item. You can see that shipment is at a different granularity than delivery.

Consequently, shipment and delivery are two different fact mini-marts related to each other, as described below. Shipment is a dedicated object in this situation, even though one source system might have shipment information directly at the delivery level. Do not make the mistake of storing shipment information received from the logistics company into shipment and small shipment information sourced from the delivery system into delivery. One is a subset of many; if your design can handle the complex situation of multiple shipments for delivery and vise-versa, then it can also take the simple one. Generalizing it makes data usage consistent, irrespective of the source system. And that's the point.

So let's dissect the above example. Below is the same model with explicit bridge tables.

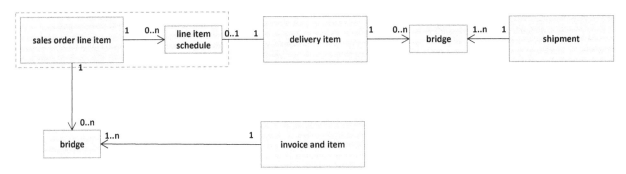

Figure 36: Example of relationships between transactional objects with bridge tables

Each object in this figure is its own fact. We have a multi-layer fact for sales orders with line items and schedule quantities, one for deliveries with their line items, one for shipments with their details, and one for invoices with their items. Logically, they are related to each other through individual bridges. But this approach requires a user to know the relationship between the objects. It also makes it cumbersome to connect sales orders with shipments. To simplify this, we use fact_affiliation and fact_ladder. Here, we briefly look at these in the context of the above example, in which we will learn more about _affiliation and _ladder in dimensions.

Fact_affiliation is a consolidation of the above bridge tables into one object. It is augmented with fact_ladder so we can directly relate any object to any other without needing to know the number or lineage of the steps in between.

```
1   CREATE TABLE IF NOT EXISTS mm22_t_supply_chain_fact_affiliation
2   (
3       preceeding_object_idd VARCHAR(64)
4       ,succeeding_object_idd VARCHAR(64)
5       ,affiliation_type VARCHAR(32)
6       ,source_system_cde VARCHAR(32)
7       , … audit fields …
8   )
9   ;
```

Sample Code 9: Sample DLL for fact affiliation

This is very similar to the _affiliation table in dimensions. Both are qualified with affiliation_type. While affiliation in dimension contains those dimensions' internal GUIDs, the unique identifier WITHIN a dimension, the affiliation between facts contains their disambiguated object_idd.

We did not address object_idd when we discussed facts like sales_order or sales_plan above, so let's do it now. Object_idd is a disambiguated natural business key for objects in mini-marts. We covered the advantages of using object_idd versus a GUID. They can be "calculated" separately in any object, like all natural business keys. They are independent of the timing of dependent objects in the enterprise data lakehouse.

Object_idd has two parts, object_id and the addition the disambiguation denoted by "d" to make object_idd. Object_idd is the disambiguated business key of the fact, a disambiguated reference to the respective fact or dimension. An example of an object_idd could be sapab.0086346778.0010, indicating line item 10 or the salesorder 0086346778 in the system sapab. Using object_idd might not look as elegant as using GUIDs but has some distinct advantages:

- fact_guid is an internal technical key within a fact. It has no business meaning. Its calculation can change or differ across source systems. It must never be exposed outside the fact.

- Our model enterprise has asynchronous global processes across different timezones. There is no guarantee that all preceding objects already exist in our data lakehouse by the time a succeeding object is received and inversely. Therefore, an ETL process cannot reliably look up for fact_guid in the respective referenced fact. Furthermore, updating a mini-mart while processing another mini-mart results in complex, entangled ETL processes leading to exponential costs and complexity.

- There is no rule in which object carries the reference to the preceding or succeeding object. Whether a delivery has references to its shipments, a shipment a reference to the deliveries, or even both. This exaggerates the look-up challenge above.

Object_idd is somewhat human-readable to someone familiar with the data. This enhances trust in the data and enables easy "sanity checks."

Lastly, object_idd is a business-defined column. Separating object_idd from fact_guid enables defining those references from a business point of view rather than a technical point of view. It might be sufficient to define object_idd as disambiguated delivery_numbers and shipment_numbers and not refer to the individual line items. This gives greater adaptability to enterprise-specific business processes.

The affiliation between facts can have a _ladder like the _ladder in dimensions. This allows for easy queries, such as "What are the shipment milestones for this sales order?" irrespective of how many layers and steps there are in between.

# SIX

# Dimensions, Synonyms, and Hierarchies

Dimensions are the other big class of mini-marts. This chapter defines a consistent blueprint for dimensions with all their real-life complexity in terms of synonyms and hierarchies.

## Overview

We stated previously that *"dimensions are pieces of data that allow you to understand and index measures in your data models. Dimensions are either characteristic of a measure or pieces of data that help contextualize the fact."* Our model organization has many such dimensions. There is likely a relatively short list of "extensive dimensions" such as material, batch, customer, employee, and others pertinent to your business and a long tail of small and potentially multilingual dimensions such as organization codes, country codes, site codes, units-of-measure, locations, property types, etc.

Each of those can have many terms for one "thing." For example, materials have many different identifiers, business partners or customers have many different codes in many different systems, and the go-to-market organization is different for each country. There might be rare cases where only one identifier exists, but one is a subset of many. If we design for "many" from the outset, we greatly reduce the risk of reworking and redesigning our datamarts. Consequently, the model should anticipate that every object has synonyms and flexible hierarchies. The former results in the _dim table, the latter in the _affiliation and _ladder tables.

Customer and vendor data are used to explain the concept. For simplification, and to make this book a bit shorter, we will just call it customer and not business partner or party, as would likely be more accurate. We will cover customer hierarchies like headquarters and branch offices. There are some implicit assumptions in the example that might not be applicable everywhere. I will try to point them out as we go along.

The complexities of multiple synonyms and others are hidden from normal data consumers. 80% of data visualization engineers and data scientists access the dimensions through simplifying views. Yet we need to dig a level deeper. The detailed tables capture the business facts irrespective of interpretation, allows for uncompromised data traceability, and mitigates changing business assumptions with little effort. In other words, they remain agile and flexible in an ever-changing environment.

Let's look at some of these complexities with some examples:

- **Synonyms have already been addressed**. Many identifiers for the same "thing". Our model enterprise has multiple transactional systems. There is no guarantee in real life that these systems are consistent among each other and have the same content. There is no guarantee that a new customer will propagate to all systems using customer data when we process data from one source. Our enterprise data lakehouse must not make any assumptions about the quality of the source data. On the contrary, the lakehouse must be able to cope with whatever ambiguous data exists and be able to reflect it as is, allowing the definition of "what correct data is" to be adjusted by the user of the data.

- **Easy consumption**. Data consumption must be easy, no matter how complex and messy our enterprise model's data. This is particularly relevant as some identifiers might be shared while others are unique. We have no control over this in a real-world environment. Assumptions we make are usually proven wrong. Often, data users are not even aware of which of the many identifiers are actually used. We use simplification views to cope with those ambiguities, avoiding the falsification of data by Cartesian products. This, in turn, allows sales, marketing, campaign, payment, and any other data from any system across the organization to be combined in integrated mini-marts in simple queries without all the complexities of source systems. This tears down silos between systems. The technique is especially helpful for customer data, for product data where there might be a variety of identifiers used across its development lifecycle, and for any other piece of information where there are historically different terms for the same thing.

- **Relationships and hierarchies within the mini-mart**. These can be organizational relationships between organizational units or the go-to-market structure, geographic relationships between places, customer hierarchies within business_partners like purchasing groups, or holdings down to branches and warehouses. Product hierarchies of any sort are a type of hierarchy. Sometimes these hierarchies are not strict hierarchies, not tree-like structures in which every node has one parent-node. Sometimes these are more like directed graphs in which any node can point to one or more other nodes and inversely. The relationships between the same object can be different depending on the viewpoint. An organization can have a legal and financial relationship between the same organizational units. Customer hierarchies can be seen from the go-to-market perspective; how customers are approached might be different from how the customer structured its organization. Any of these relationships can change over time; the go-to-market structure might be re-adjusted with every sales season to account for shifts in customer behaviors. Any such hierarchy or tree is not necessarily balanced. Hierarchies are especially useful if they can be easily queried irrespective of the number of levels. Examples might be, "Give me all organizational units that belong to XX" or "Return all customers for the holding XY, irrespective of how deep they are in the hierarchy." This is particularly helpful as the go-to-market strategy and depth of the sales organization's hierarchy might differ depending on the country. Traditionally, this results in multiple columns for each level in the hierarchy. This is rigid and assumes consistent hierarchy levels throughout the organization.

- **Multiple properties**. This is a bit of a judgment call as to whether we should treat these as individual facts or as properties of a dimension. Let's take the example of alternate units of measure or of multiple names and wordings for a material. Both are inherent properties for a material. A material is hardly complete without them and users of material master data expect such information to be "close to the material." In such a situation, we extend the dimensions directly with those properties and are not implementing them as individual fact mini-marts.

Below is the generic model for dimensions. First, we give an overview and then look at how using the data is made easy before examining each entity, its content, and the implicit assumptions or judgment calls made. We use customer just to illustrate the point, but any dimension object follows the same blueprint.

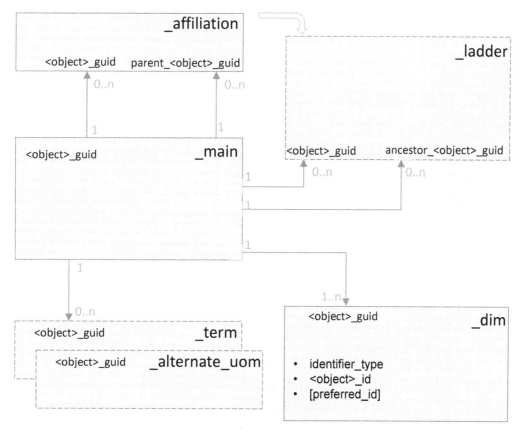

Figure 37: Generic er model for dimensions

| Entity | Content |
|---|---|
| customer_main | The core attributes of a customer, such as customer type, name, etc. Note: these entities do NOT contain the customer id. |
| customer_dim | The different identifiers for this same customer. This can be the ID in salesforce.com or in the SAP systems for the different business units of our model enterprise. |
| customer_affiliation | The relationship between customers. For example, between purchasing groups and headquarters, branches, sales offices, and contacts. This can also contain the relationship between a party and a persona in the case of a party-based model for a business partner. |
| customer_ladder | This is a derived object. It provides an easy way to find all branches, offices, and warehouses for a holding regardless of the tree's depth and the country-specific variations of our model enterprise. |
| Optional entities | Inherent properties for a customer of which there are multiples for one and the same customer. This can be a set of names or terms, key-value pairs, or any other inherent property of a dimension of which there can be many. Do not confuse those optional entities with facts, though, even if it might be a judgment call at times as to whether a property is a separate fact or part of the dimension's mini-mart. |

Figure 38: Generic entities for dimension mini-marts

# _Main

The <object>_main table contains the bulk of the information. This is the table that you naturally think about first when creating a dimension.

_main has all the attributes that are pertinent to one row or existence of the object, such as its type/subtype, its typical name/description, weight, location, and all the other things you need to know. There is one entry per "unique" existence, the unique properties of an object, no matter the number of Synonyms in _dim that an object might have. The rule is a bit different if the mini-mart is version-controlled/historized.

Note that the _main table does NOT have the *<object>_id* in there, material_main does not have material_id.

In real-world enterprises, this table ranges anywhere from seven columns to more than 200 for complex objects like product/material or customer.

Each row in this table in the mini-mart is identified by a unique <object>_GUID, except for type 2 tables. That is, tables whose content is version-controlled/historized. GUIDs are exclusively valid within a mini-mart and must not be referred to from other mini-marts/facts/dimensions.

The following is an example of a customer main table:

```
1    CREATE TABLE IF NOT EXISTS mm01_t_customer_main
2    (
3         customer_guid                 VARCHAR(32) NOT NULL
4         ,source_system_cde            VARCHAR(20)
5         ,customer_type                VARCHAR(256)
6         ,first_name                   VARCHAR(256)
7         ,middle_name                  VARCHAR(256)
8         ,last_name                    VARCHAR(256)
9         ,country_code                 CHAR(2)
10        :
11        ,all_the_other_columns        whatever it is
12        :
13   )
14   ;
```

Sample Code 10: Sample DDL for a dimension's main table

There is nothing specific about these tables other than that they do NOT have the <object>_id themselves; there is no customer_id in there. We use the field customer_guid to connect with the _customer_dim table and the other tables WITHIN this mini-mart, but never, ever to connect customers with sales data or payment data or data from any other mini-mart.

---

# _dim

In this section, we look at consistently handling synonyms.

Our model enterprise has organically grown and undergone mergers and acquisitions. Consequently, the same object, the same material or customer, business unit, or location has or can have many identifiers. The _dim table contains the list of synonyms, the list of _id that can identify any object.

There are two reasons why different identifiers might have evolved in an enterprise:

1. Additional identifiers for the same object due to object life-cycle, system necessities, or simply people's habits.

2. Consolidation of formerly disconnected systems.

We cover the latter case in more detail in the chapter about disambiguation.

The former case is very common, as some systems or business units simply had to or wanted to use a different identifier for the same object. The reasons might be that various speaking codes are used in the early development of a product to indicate the type of product, while products that are marketed later might just have a simple non-speaking number. In this case, all the identifiers used during development are synonyms of the commercial product. In the following example, we assume the same situation in which a customer might first have an identifier used in salesforce.com and later might receive an identifier used in master data and transactional SAP systems.

```
1    CREATE TABLE IF NOT EXISTS mm01_t_customer_dim
2    (
3        customer_guid              VARCHAR(32) NOT NULL
4        ,identifier_type           VARCHAR(20)
5        ,customer_id               VARCHAR(64)
6        ,source_system_cde         VARCHAR(20)
7        ,preferred_id              Boolean
8    )
9    ;
```

Sample Code 11: Sample DDL for a dimension's _dim table

All these entries are qualified with *identifier_type*. Preferred_id indicates one synonym as preferred. It is defined according to the company's business rules or preference rules.

_main and _dim are always joined when using the data in a way that avoids erroneous Cartesian products.

Obviously, this join is "preconfigured" in a view, in our case the view *mm01_customer*.

mm01_t_customer_main

| customer_guid | first_name | last_name | country_code |
|---|---|---|---|
| 900af1dd70640ca1 | Liquido | Dicuran | ES |
| c6322879a58545e2 | Granel | Racumin | PT |
| e17fdb12d20b8b9c | Dividend | Cruiser | HU |
| e240e7dde1c1a184 | Farblo | Xerotin | CH |
| ff7b9b8cba431df7 | Elatus | Seramis | CH |

Figure 39: Sample data for customer_main

The example below illustrates the heterogeneity of the identifiers in our model enterprise. We can see that the same customer can be defined in more than one system, but not necessarily in all systems. Consequently, the list of identifiers varies. Consistent use of synonyms can handle such incomplete processes and integrations. It can also cope with less-complex situations.

| first_name | country_code | exists in |
|---|---|---|
| Dividend | HU | mdm ; sapxy ; sfdc |
| Elatus | CH | mdm ; orarcp ; sapab |
| Farblo | CH | mdm ; sapab ; sapxy ; sfdc |
| Granel | PT | mdm ; sapab ; sfdc |
| Liquido | ES | mdm ; sapxy |

Figure 40: Example of heterogenous customer data

mm01_t_customer_dim

| customer_guid | source_system_cde | identifier_type | customer_id | preferred_id |
|---|---|---|---|---|
| 900af1dd70640ca1 | mdm | mdm | 825456 | TRUE |
| 900af1dd70640ca1 | mdm | sapxy | 654970123 | false |
| 900af1dd70640ca1 | sapxy | sapxy | 654970123 | false |
| c6322879a58545e2 | mdm | mdm | 1001004 | TRUE |
| c6322879a58545e2 | mdm | sapab | 140188 | false |
| c6322879a58545e2 | sapab | sapab | 140188 | false |
| c6322879a58545e2 | sfdc | salesforce | 0bf478c391f9 | false |
| c6322879a58545e2 | sfdc | sapab | 140188 | false |
| e17fdb12d20b8b9c | mdm | mdm | 38886 | TRUE |
| e17fdb12d20b8b9c | mdm | sapxy | 38886 | false |
| e17fdb12d20b8b9c | mdm | sapxy | 38886 | false |
| e17fdb12d20b8b9c | sapxy | sapxy | 38886 | false |
| e17fdb12d20b8b9c | sfdc | salesforce | 09b235ad24 | false |
| e240e7dde1c1a184 | mdm | mdm | 14807 | TRUE |
| e240e7dde1c1a184 | mdm | sapxy | 623248475 | false |
| e240e7dde1c1a184 | sapab | sapab | 107926 | false |
| e240e7dde1c1a184 | sapxy | sapxy | 623248475 | false |
| e240e7dde1c1a184 | sfdc | salesforce | 06a12c3a11b5 | false |
| e240e7dde1c1a184 | sfdc | sapab | 107926 | false |
| ff7b9b8cba431df7 | mdm | mdm | 56715 | TRUE |
| ff7b9b8cba431df7 | mdm | sapab | 4043413 | false |
| ff7b9b8cba431df7 | mdm | sapxy | 608456971 | false |
| ff7b9b8cba431df7 | orarcp | rcp | 02825dc45581 | false |
| ff7b9b8cba431df7 | sapab | sapab | 4043413 | false |

Figure 41: Sample data in a customer_dim table

Our model captures the "facts" about any object without interpretation.[32] Having full transparency might initially be complex, so using the data is simplified with a view. This example might look complex, and it is. Yet such complex data constellations exist, especially if the enterprise results from mergers and acquisitions. We are better off if the design of the

---

[32] We will cover the two classes of disambiguation in the section on Disambiguation and Qualifying.

dimensions assumes the worst. Incorporating such complexities from the outset avoids costly workarounds and rework later. Fortunately, these complexities can be completely hidden from the user, as we will see soon.

If we only did a normal join between _main and _dim we would get multiple rows with customer_id 38886, one for mdm and one for sapxy. The following view returns exactly one row for each customer_id and customer, no matter how many different or identical synonyms there are for the same customer. Note the list of identifier_types for Cruiser.

mm01_customer, the simplified view

| first_name | last_name | customer_id | identifier_type | preferred_id |
|---|---|---|---|---|
| Dividend | Cruiser | 38886 | sapxy mdm | TRUE |
| Dividend | Cruiser | 09b235ad24 | salesforce | false |
| Elatus | Seramis | 4043413 | sapab | false |
| Elatus | Seramis | 02825dc45581 | rcp | false |
| Elatus | Seramis | 56715 | mdm | TRUE |
| Elatus | Seramis | 608456971 | sapxy | false |
| Farblo | Xerotin | 06a12c3a11b5 | salesforce | false |
| Farblo | Xerotin | 107926 | sapab | false |
| Farblo | Xerotin | 14807 | mdm | TRUE |
| Farblo | Xerotin | 623248475 | sapxy | false |
| Granel | Racumin | 0bf478c391f9 | salesforce | false |
| Granel | Racumin | 1001004 | mdm | TRUE |
| Granel | Racumin | 140188 | sapab | false |
| Liquido | Dicuran | 825456 | mdm | TRUE |
| Liquido | Dicuran | 654970123 | sapxy | false |

Figure 42: How a user sees the data

We return only one row, even if the same code is a valid identifier for sapxy and for mdm. This capability is crucial as it avoids Cartesian products irrespective of the constellation and duplication of identifiers. This makes the concept robust, especially in environments where the same object can be updated and defined in multiple systems. This should not happen in theory, but in practice, it does, and the mini-marts have to cope with it, providing full transparency without losing or interpreting data.

Obviously, this flexibility has its price. We cannot beat physics. It needs more compute power to consolidate identifiers dynamically. Modern tools have that power, and many techniques exist to optimize the physical implementation and performance further. The disadvantage is outweighed by the benefit of dynamically consulting data from different, partially-overlapping source systems of complex enterprises, through the flexibility and transparency in dealing with such data. Here is the view to create this robust data:

```
1    CREATE OR REPLACE VIEW mm01_customer as
2    SELECT
3                d.customer_id
4                , d.identifier_type
5                , m.source_system_cde
6                , m.customer_type
7                , m.first_name
8                , m.middle_name
9                , m.last_name
10               , m.country_code
11               , m.all_the_other_columns
12               , m.customer_guid
13               , m.mm_create_date_time
14       FROM mm01_t_customer_main m
15       JOIN ( SELECT customer_guid
16               , customer_id
17               , btrim(listagg(DISTINCT identifier_type), ' ')
18               AS identifier_type
19               , CASE
20                     WHEN "max"(
21                     CASE
22                         WHEN preferred_id THEN 1
23                         ELSE 0
24                     END) = 1 THEN true
25                     ELSE false
26                 END AS preferred_id
27             FROM mm01_t_customer_dim
28           GROUP BY customer_guid , customer_id
29         ) d   ON m.customer_guid = d.customer_guid
30    ;
```

Sample Code 12: Simplification View for Dimensions Avoiding Cartesian Products.

Line 17 creates a list of the identifier_types. Lines 19 to 26 calculate the maximum of the Boolean column preferred_id.

# _affiliation

In this section we look at hierarchies and relationships within dimensions.

Our model enterprise has several hierarchical objects. Hierarchies are ubiquitous in any enterprise. They exist in product hierarchies, are widespread in financial reporting, and vary in go-to-market organizations. They are essential for many processes. Sometimes, they grow more complex the longer the enterprise exists. Sometimes they are balanced and have the same number of levels in all sub-trees, and sometimes they are not. The knowledge about these hierarchies occasionally exists in pockets, as with many other things in our seasoned enterprise. Our enterprise data lakehouse, or more specifically, the use of its data, must handle all this seamlessly, make different hierarchies transparent and reduce the dependency on individuals with specific knowledge.

Using hierarchies in any query is easy when the number of levels is known and balanced. It can be simply flattened out in a series of attributes or join multiple queries for each level within the hierarchy. This approach depends on the number of known and constant levels. Even this simple approach has the risk of erroneous inflation of entries for higher-level entries. These columns are repeated in the simple lists and thus occur multiple times, which might erroneously inflate related facts.

Changing such fixed hierarchies traditionally requires changes to the enterprise data warehouse and/or to the queries. While this is relatively easy within a given scope or within a given go-to-market organization for one country, it becomes trickier if we look at the entire enterprise or if we want to simulate the impact of different go-to-market organizations. It is convenient if a query can simply retrieve all sales_reps and sales_managers belonging to a specific region irrespective of whether it is a small region with just two levels or a large one with four levels of hierarchies, even imbalanced hierarchies. The approach even enables what-if analysis, dynamically changing the hierarchies and comparing the impact against each other's.

Affiliations and ladder reflect relationships within the same mini-mart. The different viewpoints are captured in the dedicated column *affiliation_type*. Such viewpoints can be legal versus financial hierarchies or specific hierarchies per business unit. *Affiliation_type* is not a placeholder for the type of customer. It does not reflect the type of any object in the relationship. These affiliations are between the entries in a mini-mart, irrespective of the synonyms or subtype of the object. Therefore, the _affiliation table contains the GUIDs of the entries, not the IDs.

To illustrate this, we use the following hypothetical relationship between the customers we used previously.

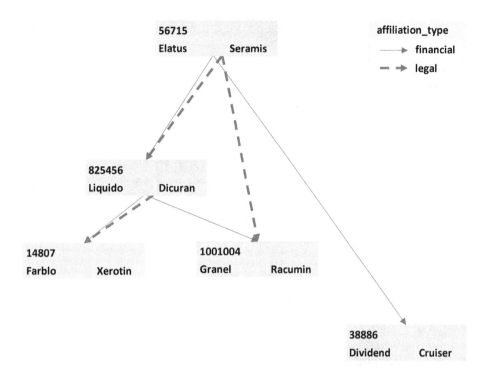

Figure 43: Example of different hierarchies within the same mini-mart

```
1   CREATE TABLE IF NOT EXISTS public_u103978.mm01_t_customer_affiliation
2   (
3       customer_guid                   VARCHAR(32) NOT NULL
4       ,parent_customer_guid           VARCHAR(32) NOT NULL
5       ,affiliation_type               VARCHAR(20)
6       ,mm_source_system_cde           VARCHAR(20)
7       ,mm_delta_hash                  VARCHAR(32)
8       ,mm_created_by                  VARCHAR(50)
9       ,mm_create_date_time            TIMESTAMP WITH TIME ZONE
10      ,mm_updated_by                  VARCHAR(50)
11      ,mm_update_date_time            TIMESTAMP WITH TIME ZONE
12  )
13  ;
```

Sample Code 13: Sample DDL for _affiliation

| parent_customer_guid | customer_guid | affiliation_type |
|---|---|---|
| 900af1dd70640ca1 | c6322879a58545e2 | financial |
| 900af1dd70640ca1 | e240e7dde1c1a184 | financial |
| ff7b9b8cba431df7 | 900af1dd70640ca1 | financial |
| ff7b9b8cba431df7 | e17fdb12d20b8b9c | financial |
| 900af1dd70640ca1 | e240e7dde1c1a184 | legal |
| ff7b9b8cba431df7 | 900af1dd70640ca1 | legal |
| ff7b9b8cba431df7 | c6322879a58545e2 | legal |

Figure 44: Sample affiliation or hierarchy data

Obviously, the data in affiliation must be combined with other data to be meaningful to the user.

```
 1    select
 2          p.customer_id , p.first_name    , a.affiliation_type
 3          , c.first_name as child_first_name  , p.customer_id
 4      from  mm01_t_customer_affiliation  a
 5      join  mm01_customer p on a.parent_customer_guid = p.customer_guid
 6                          and p.preferred_id
 7      join  mm01_customer c on a.customer_guid       = c.customer_guid
 8                          and c.preferred_id
 9      order by affiliation_type, a.parent_customer_guid desc , a.customer_guid
10        ;
```

Sample Code 14: Combining affiliations with other data

We can see the use of preferred_id above to prevent Cartesian products. Alternatively, a specific identifier_type could be selected.

This results in the same information in tabular form as depicted in the graph.

| customer_id | first_name | affiliation_type | child_first_name | customer_id |
|---|---|---|---|---|
| 56715 | Elatus | financial | Liquido | 56715 |
| 56715 | Elatus | financial | Dividend | 56715 |
| 825456 | Liquido | financial | Granel | 825456 |
| 825456 | Liquido | financial | Farblo | 825456 |
| 56715 | Elatus | legal | Liquido | 56715 |
| 56715 | Elatus | legal | Granel | 56715 |
| 825456 | Liquido | legal | Farblo | 825456 |

Figure 45: Tabular data of the sample customer hierarchy

# _ladder

This chapter teaches us how to query easily, even for members in dynamic and unbalanced hierarchies.

Affiliations are just one level of hierarchies at a time, albeit over many steps in succession. The real ease of use comes when we can query the data irrespective of the number of levels in any hierarchy, in simple ways, and even in unbalanced trees. For this, we use _ladder. It allows for queries without needing to know the depth of the hierarchy. This makes it applicable in dynamic, heterogenous environments such as the various go-to-market organizations in our model enterprise.

Let's pretend we have sales regions and below them sales territories. In some countries, sales territories are further divided into sales districts and, ultimately, into sales offices. Key customers might be served directly by the sales territory or even region, while the sales office serves smaller customers. Every year, this sales structure is refined to account for demographics and customer behavior changes. But of course, we want to compare this year's sales for "my" sales territory irrespective of the sales organization "my" customers were assigned last year. The concept of _ladder enables us to do this easily, returning all customers of the current sales hierarchy irrespective of the previous assignment, with no need to adjust historical data.

To illustrate the concept, the same customer data is used as for _affiliation. We add additional columns to make the use of it easier. These are the _IDs [ancestor_customer_id and customer_id] and distance, the depth of the tree between the ancestor, leaf object, and customer_id_path, and a column indicating the full hierarchy path. This column is added for illustration only, to increase transparency, help understand sometimes surprising data and clarify how a given object is related to the ancestor.

We can see a few details in _ladder, such as the distance and each row referring to itself as ancestor [distance = 0]. While this might be puzzling initially, it allows for very simple and resilient queries in complex and unbalanced hierarchies. In the previous example, the complete ladder data is as follows:

mm01_ladder

| affiliation_type | ancestor guid and name | distance | customer_id_path | leaf guid and name |
|---|---|---|---|---|
| financial | e17fdb12d20b8b9c Dividend | 0 | > 38886 | e17fdb12d20b8b9c Dividend |
| financial | ff7b9b8cba431df7 Elatus | 0 | > 56715 | ff7b9b8cba431df7 Elatus |
| financial | ff7b9b8cba431df7 Elatus | 1 | > 56715> 38886 | e17fdb12d20b8b9c Dividend |
| financial | ff7b9b8cba431df7 Elatus | 1 | > 56715> 825456 | 900af1dd70640ca1 Liquido |
| financial | ff7b9b8cba431df7 Elatus | 2 | > 56715> 825456> 14807 | e240e7dde1c1a184 Farblo |
| financial | ff7b9b8cba431df7 Elatus | 2 | > 56715> 825456> 1001004 | c6322879a58545e2 Granel |
| financial | e240e7dde1c1a184 Farblo | 0 | > 14807 | e240e7dde1c1a184 Farblo |
| financial | c6322879a58545e2 Granel | 0 | > 1001004 | c6322879a58545e2 Granel |
| financial | 900af1dd70640ca1 Liquido | 0 | > 825456 | 900af1dd70640ca1 Liquido |
| financial | 900af1dd70640ca1 Liquido | 1 | > 825456> 14807 | e240e7dde1c1a184 Farblo |
| financial | 900af1dd70640ca1 Liquido | 1 | > 825456> 1001004 | c6322879a58545e2 Granel |
| legal | e17fdb12d20b8b9c Dividend | 0 | > 38886 | e17fdb12d20b8b9c Dividend |
| legal | ff7b9b8cba431df7 Elatus | 0 | > 56715 | ff7b9b8cba431df7 Elatus |
| legal | ff7b9b8cba431df7 Elatus | 1 | > 56715> 1001004 | c6322879a58545e2 Granel |
| legal | ff7b9b8cba431df7 Elatus | 1 | > 56715> 825456 | 900af1dd70640ca1 Liquido |
| legal | ff7b9b8cba431df7 Elatus | 2 | > 56715> 825456> 14807 | e240e7dde1c1a184 Farblo |
| legal | e240e7dde1c1a184 Farblo | 0 | > 14807 | e240e7dde1c1a184 Farblo |
| legal | c6322879a58545e2 Granel | 0 | > 1001004 | c6322879a58545e2 Granel |
| legal | 900af1dd70640ca1 Liquido | 0 | > 825456 | 900af1dd70640ca1 Liquido |
| legal | 900af1dd70640ca1 Liquido | 1 | > 825456> 14807 | e240e7dde1c1a184 Farblo |

Figure 46: Example of complete_ladder data

_ladder allows simple queries to return all entries belonging to a particular parent entry, no matter the number of levels, within a given context, also known as affiliation_type. This is a stark departure from traditional implementations of fixed column hierarchies.

The below example returns all children of Elatus irrespective of their distance or number of levels in between. It can be done in one simple statement. Doing the same with _affiliation would require as many consecutive joins as there are levels in between.

```
1    select
2          parent.first_name
3          , l.distance , l.affiliation_type
4          , child.first_name, child.country_code
5          , l.customer_id_path
6      from mm01_customer child
7      join mm01_customer_ladder l
                    on l.customer_guid   = child.customer_guid
8                    and child.preferred_id
9      join mm01_customer parent
                    on l.ancestor_customer_guid = parent.customer_guid
10                   and parent.preferred_id
11     where parent.first_name = 'Elatus'
12       and l.affiliation_type = 'legal'
13     order by l.distance , child.customer_id ;
```

Sample Code 15: List of entire hierarchy irrespective of number of levels in between

| first_name | distance | affiliation_type | first_name | country_code | customer_id_path[33] |
|---|---|---|---|---|---|
| Elatus | 0 | legal | Elatus | CH | > 56715 |
| Elatus | 1 | legal | Granel | PT | > 56715> 1001004 |
| Elatus | 1 | legal | Liquido | ES | > 56715> 825456 |
| Elatus | 2 | legal | Farblo | CH | > 56715> 825456> 14807 |

Figure 47: Sample of dependent entries

Note that this query did not return "Dividend" as this "Dividend" is only financial, but not legally a direct or indirect child or "Elatus."

The next example is a bit more interesting. It combines the power of synonyms with the elegance of ladder to calculate the total sales for an entire customer hierarchy irrespective of the number of levels, the balancing of the hierarchy, or the specific customer identifier used.

---

[33] This column is for illustration purposes.

```
1    SELECT s.customer_id, c.first_name , s.mm_source_system
2         ,sum(s.quantity) as sales_quantity_sum
3      from mm03_salesorder_fact s
4      join mm01_customer        c on s.customer_id = c.customer_id
5      where s.customer_id in
6         (select d.customer_id
7              from mm01_customer_ladder l
8              join mm01_t_customer_dim  d
9                   on l.customer_guid = d.customer_guid
10             join mm01_customer parent
11                  on l.ancestor_customer_guid = parent.customer_guid
12             where parent.first_name = 'Elatus'
13                and l.affiliation_type = 'legal' )
14     group by 1,2,3
15     order by 2,1
```

Sample Code 16: Querying an unbalanced tree regardless of synonym

It reports the sales data from below entries for a total of 216.

| customer_id | first_name | mm_source_system | sales_quantity_sum |
|---|---|---|---|
| 02825dc45581 | Elatus | rcp | 111 |
| 4043413 | Elatus | sapab | 11 |
| 107926 | Farblo | sapab | 44 |
| 140188 | Granel | sapab | 22 |
| 825456 | Liquido | sapab | 28 |
| | | | 216 |

Figure 48: Samples sales data for a complete hierarchy at once

The query returns the sales quantities for Seramis/Elatus from both source systems, from SAPAB, and from rcp. This is despite these systems using different identifiers for the same customer. Sales from Dividend/Cruiser are not included. These are only financially, yet not legally, a direct or indirect child of Seramis/Elatus. The result is not dependent on the depth and balance of the customer hierarchy, adapting easily to changing hierarchies and systems.

_ladder itself is derived from _affiliation. Some database technologies allow for recursive views. Other technologies need ladder derived explicitly from _affiliation via a dedicated ETL script that loops over successive affiliations. Below is an example of the recursive view for _ladder. The view is enriched with tracing information like the customer_id_path. Such information is helpful as it increases transparency and hence trust in the data.

```
1   create or replace view mm01_customer_ladder as
2   with recursive customer_hierarchy
3                   (ancestor_customer_guid
4                   , customer_id_path
5                   , customer_guid
6                   , affiliation_type
7                   , distance ) as
8      (
9         select  m.customer_guid                    as ancestor_customer_guid
10                ,''::varchar(65000)                as customer_id_path
11                ,m.customer_guid                   as customer_guid
12                ,a.affiliation_type
13                , 0                                as distance
14            from mm01_t_customer_main    m
15            join mm01_t_customer_dim     d
16              on m.customer_guid = d.customer_guid  and d.preferred_id
17            join (select distinct affiliation_type
18                    from mm01_t_customer_affiliation
19                  ) a on 1=1 -- create the complete list of affiliation_types
20        union all
21        select
22                h.ancestor_customer_guid              as ancestor_customer_guid
23               ,customer_id_path || '> ' || d.customer_id as customer_id_path
24               ,a.customer_guid                       as customer_guid
25               ,a.affiliation_type
26               ,distance + 1                          as distance
27           from mm01_t_customer_affiliation a
28           join mm01_t_customer_dim     d
29             on a.parent_customer_guid = d.customer_guid
30             and d.preferred_id
31           join customer_hierarchy                h
32             on h.customer_guid = a.parent_customer_guid
33             and h.affiliation_type = a.affiliation_type
34           join mm01_t_customer_main    m on a.parent_customer_guid = m.customer_guid
35           where distance < 9
36      )
37   select
38         h.affiliation_type                      as affiliation_type
39        , h.ancestor_customer_guid               as ancestor_customer_guid
40        ,h.distance                              as distance
41        ,h.customer_id_path || '> ' || dl.customer_id  as customer_id_path
42        ,h.customer_guid                         as customer_guid
43     from  customer_hierarchy h
44     join  mm01_t_customer_dim dl
45       on dl.customer_guid = h.customer_guid          and dl.preferred_id
46      ;
```

Sample Code 17: Sample Code for Recursive _Ladder View

# Additional information

This chapter deals with the wealth of "other information" any real-life object has.

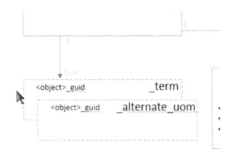

Figure 49: Additional information for dimensions

A dimension such as customer [business partners, vendors, party], materials [products], and places [locations] often has additional information attached to it that must be available in the enterprise data mart.

These entities refer to "one and the same thing," one entry in _main, to the same customer and to the same product. Examples can be a long list of potential names and descriptions, various alternate units-of-measure, different properties of the "same thing" in different regions, systems, and many others. Another typical example are key/value pairs, such as classification in SAP. They must not be confused with "facts," although it might sometimes be a judgment call.

It is futile to overengineer these entities. Often they are too dynamic and diverse, so we use pragmatic solutions to minimize maintenance costs. They are implemented in classical entity relationship form, as additional tables within the dimension mini-mart linked via a joint _GUID. They are included in queries as needed. Just be wary of not creating Cartesian products when using them.

Below is an example of such an additional table for material, containing the various names and terms a material might have in many different languages, sometimes specific to sales organizations or distribution channels.

```
1    CREATE TABLE IF NOT EXISTS mm04_t_material_term
2    (
3        material_guid                VARCHAR(64)
4        ,identifier_type             VARCHAR(50)
5        ,identifier_subtype          VARCHAR(50)
6        ,term                        VARCHAR(600)
7        ,language_code               CHAR(2)
8        ,distribution_channel_idd    VARCHAR(20)
9        ,sales_org_cde               VARCHAR(20)
10       ,mm_delta_hash               VARCHAR(64)
11       ,mm_source_system            VARCHAR(20)
12       ,mm_create_date_time         TIMESTAMP
13       ,mm_update_date_time         TIMESTAMP
14       ,mm_created_by               VARCHAR(100)
15       ,mm_updated_by               VARCHAR(100)
16   )
17   ;
```

Sample Code 18: Sample DDL for different names for a material

## Consolidation

This section will cover consolidating multiple data sources into a unified dataset.

It is easier for users to filter for a data subset than it is to search for a different mart with similar data. In other words, it is very transparent for users to filter on mm_source_system for the data subset they need explicitly, or not to filter at all if they need consolidated numbers. This is easier than searching for all source-system-specific copies of a mini-mart in the hopes of obtaining a total of consolidated numbers. It simplifies the query. The query does not need to combine data from multiple mini-marts for a consolidated view.

Such is the power of consolidated mini-marts and making implicit knowledge explicit.

Consolidating for facts is essentially just each source system adding "its rows" to a joint mini-mart, with columns aligned by business meaning and every record qualified with source_system and any other qualifying column required. While consolidation comes easy for fact data, consolidation is a bit trickier for dimensions. There are two fundamentally different approaches to this consolidation: hard and soft consolidation. The choice between them is business-driven. In short, use hard consolidation if you are certain that the entry with the same key really means the same "thing" in all systems and soft consolidation if you are not so sure.

## Hard consolidation

We used hard consolidation in our customer example in Figure 42. This approach is applicable if a rigorous process guarantees data consistency across the various systems, even though the same entry might have different identifiers or synonyms. Hard consolidation is possible if at least some systems carry some parts of the cross-reference in various combinations, yet the data content is consistent across all systems. Sometimes this cross-reference might only exist in a niche system, but in most cases, they exist.

In hard consolidation, each entry has exactly one entry in _main. We dynamically derive this single object_guid from a matching synonym in _dim or create it if it does not already exist. Ultimately, each entry has one row in _main and as many synonyms in _dim as there are across the various systems.

## Soft consolidation

The customer example used was based on hard consolidation. Now we will compare it with soft consolidation. Customer, at least in theory, should originate from one system only. In reality, customer data and its identifiers are sometimes locally-created in a marketing system and sometimes locally modified in go-to-market systems. Our enterprise data lakehouse must not make any assumptions about the congruence of data. In such situations, one can never be sure that the same set of customer_ids in one system really means the same and matches the data from another source. On the other hand, we must guarantee that every customer_id existing returns exactly one record to avoid erroneous Cartesian products when joining facts with the customer dimension.

Moreover, customer data consolidation might add additional dynamics. We can use soft consolidation for such conditions, making it more dynamic and flexible for the price of more compute-intensive queries.

Your customer data might look like what appears in the following list. First_name is spelled differently in some systems. You can picture any data deviating between different systems. Obviously, an attempt to consolidate the data could be made. This is a long process, especially in large enterprises. It is also difficult to sustain. It might be easier to accept the data as it is and use the data lakehouse's capabilities for transparency.

The example assumes each system has a partial copy of customer data with a subset of its various identifiers. There is no guarantee that either of these lists is consistent or complete. Errors and local modifications happen, although most data is at least not contradicting other data.

There are as many entries in _main for potentially the "same partner" as there are relevant source systems, hence "Soft consolidation." Note the occasionally different spelling of some first names, used to exemplify data inconsistency.

| customer_guid | source_system_cde | first_name | last_name | identifier_type | customer_id |
|---|---|---|---|---|---|
| ee9f65d1e12f8e5a | mdm | Dividend | Cruiser | mdm | 38886 |
| | | | | salesforce | 09b235ad24 |
| | | | | sapxy | 38886 |
| dea3b6ce641066c9 | sapxy | Dividend | Cruiser | sapxy | 38886 |
| cde88ca98c2262b5 | sfdc | Divident as spelled in sfdc | Cruiser | salesforce | 09b235ad24 |
| 1d7090ca399b393b | orarcp | Elatus | Seramis | mdm | 56715 |
| | | | | rcp | 02825dc45581 |
| | | | | sapab | 4043413 |
| | | | | sapxy | 608456971 |
| 3302788807c5411c | sapab | Elatus | Seramis | sapab | 4043413 |
| a2a60900ae6bd196 | mdm | Elatuzz as spelled in MDM | Seramis | mdm | 56715 |
| | | | | sapab | 4043413 |
| | | | | sapxy | 608456971 |
| 3f1c0651c4bb76e2 | mdm | Farblo | Xerotin | mdm | 14807 |
| | | | | salesforce | 06a12c3a11b5 |
| | | | | sapab | 107926 |
| | | | | sapxy | 623248475 |
| 79df4dd50eabe302 | sapab | Farblo | Xerotin | sapab | 107926 |
| 95aeda4557f33270 | sfdc | Farblo | Xerotin | salesforce | 06a12c3a11b5 |
| | | | | sapab | 107926 |
| 534699b25abe63d7 | sapxy | Farxy as spelled in sapxy | Xerotin | sapxy | 623248475 |
| 982bd3ebf62d154e | mdm | Granel | Racumin | mdm | 1001004 |
| | | | | salesforce | 0bf478c391f9 |
| | | | | sapab | 140188 |
| 5ac04047dc93e09d | sapab | Granel | Racumin | sapab | 140188 |
| 0b0506718a507a7d | sfdc | Granel | Racumin | salesforce | 0bf478c391f9 |
| | | | | sapab | 140188 |
| d6aa7178a8eec857 | mdm | Liquido | Dicuran | mdm | 825456 |
| | | | | sapxy | 654970123 |
| 1c22bed5c46d2b17 | sapxy | Liquido | Dicuran | sapxy | 654970123 |

Figure 50: Example of incoherent customer data

Soft consolidation is relevant to understanding a customer, even in incoherent, fragmented environments. It is substantially more challenging, both in concept and in use. Soft Consolidation is, in essence, a "dynamic golden record" while always preserving the full transparency and reconciliation of its details. We might use soft consolidation in environments with limited process control or where customers are created separately in various processes. Some types of customers will be consolidated later into a coherent master data entry. Even those might be locally modified again. You might encounter an environment in which several attempts have been made to consolidate customer master data. All of them were successful in their respective domains, yet it is very difficult to cover all customers in a dynamic environment. For example, local sub-processes could change, such as creating leads that later became customers. This is where soft consolidation might be appropriate.

Handling soft consolidation is far too complex for "normal data consumers." That is why it hides in a view. This guarantees exactly one row for every *customer_id,* no matter the data inconsistencies. Consolidation between "identical entries," also known as supposedly identical customers, is done through the same identifier and identifier_type existing in different systems. The preference rule for "the one entry" depends on business definitions and trust level. We preserve the ability to analyze details. A few takeaways from the example below:

- Every customer_id is returned exactly once.

- The preference rule first returns the content of the source system of which the identifier_type is native (data from sapab if identifier_type is sapab).

- If there is no such entry (the "Seramis" example from sapab) then it returns data from mdm. In theory, such cases should not exist, yet they might. For example, if the entry had been deleted in one system while related historical data exists elsewhere (or simply through data synchronization errors).

- The column source_system_cdes [plural] lists all systems in which this customer_id exists. This is helpful for data consistency diagnosis.

| customer_id | identifier_type | source_system_cde | source_system_cdes | first_name | last_name |
|---|---|---|---|---|---|
| 38886 | sapxy | sapxy | mdm , sapxy | Dividend | Cruiser |
| 09b235ad24 | salesforce | sfdc | mdm , sfdc | Divident as spelled in sfdc | Cruiser |
| 02825dc45581 | rcp | orarcp | orarcp | Elatus | Seramis |
| 4043413 | sapab | sapab | mdm , orarcp , sapab | Elatus | Seramis |
| 56715 | mdm | mdm | mdm , orarcp | Elatuzz as spelled in MDM | Seramis |
| 608456971 | sapxy | mdm | mdm , orarcp | Elatuzz as spelled in MDM | Seramis |
| 14807 | mdm | mdm | mdm | Farblo | Xerotin |
| 06a12c3a11b5 | salesforce | sfdc | mdm , sfdc | Farblo | Xerotin |
| 107926 | sapab | sapab | mdm , sapab , sfdc | Farblo | Xerotin |
| 623248475 | sapxy | sapxy | mdm , sapxy | Farxy as spelled in sapxy | Xerotin |
| 1001004 | mdm | mdm | mdm | Granel | Racumin |
| 0bf478c391f9 | salesforce | sfdc | mdm , sfdc | Granel | Racumin |
| 140188 | sapab | sapab | mdm , sapab , sfdc | Granel | Racumin |
| 825456 | mdm | mdm | mdm | Liquido | Dicuran |
| 654970123 | sapxy | sapxy | mdm , sapxy | Liquido | Dicuran |

Figure 51: Sample soft consolidated data

The "party approach" might be one way out of this dilemma whereby an affiliation is maintained between the "consolidated party" and different instances, also known as personas, of the "same customer."[34] Did you notice affiliation in the above sentence? The relationship between "party" and its personas is, in fact, an affiliation between different types of entries. Party data and persona data are the data that are preferentially returned but supplemented by any other data in case of deviations or gaps.

Implementing a global party concept requires considerable effort. Soft consolidation in the mini-marts allows for approximation without the deep process impact. Of course, there is never a free lunch, so it is a best-effort approach to provide enough additional information to identify and reason data inconsistencies. It enables continuous source data quality improvement by attrition.

Alternate rules and complete traceability to the source are always possible. The complete set of underlying data and relationships is still available. It is hidden and not needed in 80% of the use cases.

To show the full picture, here is the view behind the above example:

---

[34] https://www.stibosystems.com/blog/what-you-need-to-know-about-party-data.

```
1   create view mm11_customer
2   -- a sample view for soft consolidating customer data
3   as select
4         customer_guid
5         ,c.customer_id
6         ,identifier_type
7         ,source_system_cde
8         ,source_system_cdes
9         ,first_name
10        ,last_name
11    from (
12          SELECT
13                  d.customer_guid
14                  ,d.customer_id
15                  ,d.identifier_type
16                  ,m.source_system_cde
17                  ,m.first_name
18                  ,m.last_name
19                  ,row_number() over (partition by d.customer_id
20                    order by case
21                      when m.source_system_cde = d.identifier_type   then 0
22                      when m.source_system_cde =
                              decode(d.identifier_type , 'salesforce','sfdc',
                                                         'rcp','orarcp','n/a') then 1
23                    else nvl(t.priority, 100)
24                    end    ) as rn
25              from mm11_t_customer_dim   d
26              join mm11_t_customer_main m on m.customer_guid = d.customer_guid
27              left join
28                  (select 'mdm' AS source_system_cde, 99 AS priority) t
29                        on t.source_system_cde = m.source_system_cde
30          ) c
31    join (select customer_id
32                , listagg(distinct source_system_cde, ' , ')
33                  within group (order by source_system_cde) as source_system_cdes
34              from mm11_t_customer_dim
35              group by 1
36          ) s on s.customer_id = c.customer_id
37      where rn=1
38        ;
```

Sample Code 20: View for Soft Consolidation

## Disambiguation and qualifying

This section will examine cases in which the same "code value" means different things in different systems. One example might be a sales office whose abbreviation in one system or region means something completely different in another.

Using extended natural business keys instead of GUIDs is not a textbook procedure, and data purists will rightfully criticize it. They prefer GUIDs. This is undoubtedly correct for transactional systems. However, internal technical keys of transactional systems should never be exposed and used outside the original transactional system. Our data lakehouse must solely rely on data that is exposed by the source system for external usage. GUIDs for joining between objects in our data lakehouse would need to be calculated in the data lakehouse. This would require a look-up to retrieve the GUIDs from dependent objects. This, in turn, creates dependencies and threatens the independence of data mesh nodes. GUIDs would not solve any problems other than lack of aesthetics while making everything more complex. The business rules and challenges for determining GUIDs remain the same.

Using business keys is more transparent and understandable for the user. But most importantly, extended natural business keys allow for asynchronous processes across different systems, data mesh nodes, and time zones. Different conventions in the data mesh nodes are neatly handled by the synonyms inherent to the design. They are almost a prerequisite for a truly federated yet collaborative data mesh.

Any organization operating for some time has a substantial set of implicit assumptions in every function. These can be terms that have a specific meaning. A good example is "plant," which refers to green things growing in a field or a factory as in "manufacturing plant." There are plenty of other terms that have specific meanings. "Open order" might mean different things to different parts of an organization. It can mean "not confirmed," "not delivered," or "not invoiced." Sometimes, such and other assumptions are implicitly embedded in the data source itself, like "data comes from a particular system" or "the filename contains the year." In any case, such implicit assumptions must be explicit in the mini-mart, either by qualifying the column name, adding additional qualifying columns, or qualifying the content of the columns. Any of these transform implicit knowledge into explicit content.

Our model enterprise has many different transactional and other systems. Our mini-marts are highly-generalized, consolidated data from various systems. They are based on natural business keys, namely the _IDs in the above _dim tables. When combined, there is no guarantee that one and the same value for one key [_id] means the same everywhere.

This is where disambiguation and qualifying are needed. We use disambiguation when the same <code> for the same object means different things in different source systems. One example can be the sales office in SAP. Code 1101 means something completely different in one system than the same code 1101 means in another system. These can be qualified, resulting in sapab.1101 and sapxy.1101, respectively. We use qualifying identifiers when generalization combines "things" that were previously different but could potentially have the same <code>. An example of this could be when generalizing hierarchies to make them flexible. Code 34 can be a sales group or a sales office, so it is qualified as salesgroup.34 and salesoffice.34, respectively.

Disambiguation extends ambiguous columns [_ids] with the reference system or other differentiators to make their content globally unique. Disambiguation only applies to those objects whose _id is ambiguous.

Giving disambiguated keys a dedicated naming convention is good practice. For example, _idd for "_id- disambiguated." In the previous customer example, we assumed that the customer_id(s) are different between SAPAB and SAPXY systems or between those systems and MDM. We used the customer_id column as it is. Business analysts and a careful analysis of the data will clarify whether this assumption of uniqueness is correct.

This column must be disambiguated if the same code can mean different customers in different systems. This column content might be 'sapab.140188' or 'mdm.38886'. We use *customer_idd* instead of *customer_id*.

There is an important caution, though. Disambiguation is based on the reference system and not on the source system. Let's assume a Point-of-Sales System (POSS) is connected to our SAPAB system. Our business analyst will tell us that the sales-data's customer_ids in the POSS system are, in fact, SAPAB codes. Therefore, the customer_id from the POSS must be disambiguated with *SAPAB...* and not with *POSS...* although the source for the data is the POSS system.

Qualifying can be relevant if hierarchies are generalized, as in the above example of salesoffice and salesgroup. Qualifying is also needed to align between different systems, such as traditional column-based hierarchies like in SAP with the dynamic hierarchies in salesforce.com.

Other examples include places or locations. There are many different types of "places," such as weather station positions, nodes on a weather grid, or the location of a city, port, farmer's field, or field trial. These are all different subtypes of *Places*. We saw previously in _affiliation that we can generalize potentially imbalanced and flexible hierarchies, affording more flexibility in adjusting them. The downside is that those IDs need to be qualified.

Such qualifications can be pragmatic, as we've seen above for salesoffice and salesgroup. Using a different example, Location.un.USKDD is the UN-location-based identifier for Kadoka, SD in the US, US.postal.57543 would be its ZIP-based identifier. gridpoint_-006.50000_-047.05000 identifies a weather grid, PT.postal.8500-507 is Portimão in Portugal for its postal code. Don't become dogmatic on the qualifications of identifiers. They only must be unique and documented in the data catalog.

It might be difficult for data engineers to cope with such open definitions, as they prefer GUIDs. But the questions about "what unique is" remain the same, just hidden. Using those qualifiers openly does not win you a prize for looks, but it does add transparency and pragmatism, ultimately allowing for independence across mini-marts and across the data mesh.

# SEVEN

# ETL Simplifications

This chapter discusses techniques to populate the mini-marts and accompanying sample codes to accelerate their implementation.

## Data virtualization versus data lakehouse

There are different techniques for physically integrating data: data virtualization versus integration, such as co-located marts or data lakehouses. The former leaves the data where it originates in the source systems and puts layers above it, mimicking a consolidated view across multiple source systems. The latter co-locates the data from the various source systems into one common technical platform or across a data mesh. There are gray zones in between and many marketing buzzwords to obfuscate the concepts. But it is hard to beat physics and basic principles.

There are pros and cons to these approaches. The data model concepts proposed in this book can work with both. They do not make assumptions about either approach. We can virtually transform the source system data into the integrated models proposed here. After all, all mini-marts are independent of each other and can be highly parallelized.

The key argument in favor of data virtualization is the elimination of data duplication. However, I prefer co-locating data in one physical place. Often data needs to be replicated anyway to be useable for data analysis for these reasons:

- OLTP vs. OLAP: transactional source systems use an OLTP data model unsuitable for the analytical processing of large amounts of data. For this reason, data still needs to be copied into an OLAP environment.

- Load on source systems: owners of source systems are not very enthusiastic when it comes to regularly reading large amounts of data from their system. Well-designed data marts retrieve changed source system data once only, not large amounts repeatedly.

Physically co-locating data in one place is predominantly an organizational question and yields benefits for combining data. Joining data within one platform is well established and optimized by the database management system. Joining data from physically distributed marts implies loading one data set and combining it in the background with the matching pieces from another data set. Co-locating data allows the database management system to optimize these joins efficiently. Data virtualization does not have the same options if data is located on different platforms. Data caching and other techniques can optimize this somewhat, but these are hidden data loads, which is merely another way of co-locating data.

For these reasons, this book assumes that the data is co-located in one form or another. We can apply some of these examples to data virtualization. The code samples are in AWS Redshift. However, any other columnar store will do as well. I use SQL to illustrate some of the concepts. It is highly transparent, relatively condensed, and widely known. It avoids the layer of obfuscation from metadata-driven approaches, enables complex rules to be expressed if necessary, and allows the database's optimizer to deploy its full potential. Additionally, it enables verification of the data together with the business owner very early in the development process, thereby reducing error costs and speeding up implementation. Obviously, there are other techniques. Ultimately, it is the outcome that matters. The "what," not the "how." The techniques used here are just for illustration.

## ETL principles

In this section we look at pragmatic yet robust and efficient ETL processes.

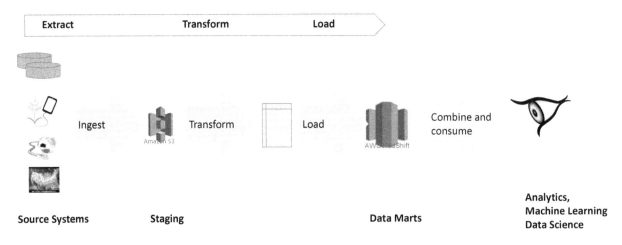

Figure 52: Basic ETL process

ETL (Extract, Transform, and Load) and ELT (Extract, Load, and Transform) can be done regularly, for example, hourly, daily, or continuously. The examples below assume a regular update as this is best suited for explaining the process. The process for streaming data is similar but might use different technologies for ingestion and might assume that no data is received twice.

ETL processes must be:

- **Robust and prevent duplications**. This sounds obvious and trivial. Nevertheless, the data lakehouse has no control over the data it receives. Any source can send the same data more than once. No input data can push the datamart into an inconsistent state. This implies that the ETL process is robust for the same data received multiple times. It must prevent accidental data duplication. A source system must not need to know whether some data has already been sent and successfully processed. Processes can be fully decoupled, and there is no need to logically differentiate between initial, reconciliation, delta, or even overlapping delta loads. This greatly simplifies the operation.

- **Delta load**. Only changed source data. That is, we need delta data to feed into the ETL processes, a full load at most for very small data sets. While this sounds nice in theory, not all source systems can provide delta data. If the source system cannot provide delta, then the ETL processes should minimize the number of write operations.

- **Self-correcting**. Mistakes happen, and Murphy was an optimist. It will happen that processes fail and data goes missing. It must be possible to trigger "broad scope" reconciliation loads or re-loads without needing to analyze the individual missing data in detail. In other words, if mistakes happen, then entire "chunks" of data can be re-loaded without analyzing the individual missing records.

- **Transparent**. ETL processes must be transparent and easy to maintain, and all transformation should be concentrated in "one place." Avoid spreading transformations across different technologies and modules. As the saying goes, the fewer modules you need to change, the more agile the process.

## Ingestion

In this section, we get data from the source to the "delivery gate" for our data lakehouse.

Extraction from the source, also known as ingestion into the staging area, is driven mainly by the technologies available to retrieve data from sources and less by the technology of the data lakehouse. A one-size-fits-all approach is rarely possible. You should select the techniques and technologies best suited to your environment.

Optional techniques and/or tools are:[35]

- Kafka pipelines

- API calls to source

- Database replication services

- Messaging from classical message middleware

- Access to the source database

- Tools like Business Objects Data Services, Snaplogic, Talend, and others

- Old-fashioned file transfer

There must not be any assumption about ingestion processing other than:

- Ultimately all data is transmitted at least once.

- Data arrives in approximately chronological order or at least has a timestamp allowing it to be chronologically sorted.

Other assumptions like "data is transmitted exactly once" will be proven wrong in practice. ETL processes building on such assumptions will occasionally fail and are difficult to reconcile. Always assume the worst and plan for the worst.

Let's look at the above techniques in more detail. Message-based technologies are a great means for ingestion, especially if messages are published anyway as part of transactional processes and can be reused. However, the messages must be atomic, the messaging service must be reliable, and re-publishing must be triggerable if a rectification load is needed. "Atomic" means the complete object exists within the message. A "complete object" means a complete sales order or a complete product and not just fragments of it. "Reliable" means that all changes at the source trigger messages, and no message gets lost in between. Re-publishing is needed in case something goes wrong. When planning for message-based technologies, consider whether reconciliation loads are possible for re-publishing large sets of data objects again.

Messages must be atomic/complete and properly timestamped. Message-based technologies might send multiple messages for the same object within any given period. Transformation and load must cope with multiple messages for the same object and prevent erroneously duplicated data in the mini-marts.

---

[35] Some of the options listed are techniques and some are tools; their capabilities are partially overlapping.

Polling API calls to retrieve changed data from source systems might be a good method if there is low-volume data[36] and if APIs exist for retrieving changed entries. Design for robustness. Data extraction will inevitably go wrong from time to time. A successful API call does not necessarily guarantee a successful data load into the mini-marts. The parameter for what "changed data" is, or more precisely "data changed since," must not be controlled by the source system but by the consuming system, the ETL process for loading data. Extracting data by direct access to the source database might not be the most elegant approach, but it is often the simplest and thus the most robust one. It is transparent especially if the source system's owner provides a view that is preparing the relevant data. Other approaches might be technologies like Iceberg.

Consider the robustness of delta data in non-streaming environments. In theory, data never goes missing and everything is watertight and perfect. If not, ensure missing data is loaded automatically on the next occasion. If the data volume allows it, be pragmatic. If changed data is retrieved every two hours, you may retrieve data changed in the last five hours to ensure that a missed heartbeat is rectified on the next load, and likewise for daily schedules.

---

# Transform

In this section, we transform the raw data into a simplified form so mini-marts can easily integrate with each other.

Transform is the core of the data pipeline. The "business knowledge" is captured in this process. Some code samples are listed hereafter. Every mini-mart adheres to a conformed design and naming standard, irrespective of its technical source. This harmonization occurs in the transform step. The transform step condenses the application-specific tables of the source system into business meaning. It translates it into a form that is easy to understand and query. Transform results in an intermediary table that is subsequently loaded into the mini-mart while preventing duplicates, performing historicization, and maintaining consistent atomic lists.

Transform involves:

- renaming technical column names to business speaking names. Doing this in the transform step only makes it more transparent and easier to maintain.

- denormalizing data into facts and multi-layer facts, the easy-to-use mini-marts.

- standardizing dimensions including their affiliations.

---

[36] Low-volume: a few million entries a day.

- conforming and disambiguating identifiers, the conformed dimensions in natural business keys.

- calculating the GUIDs used within, but never outside of, an individual mini-mart.

- eliminating potentially duplicative source data, especially in message-based feeds. It should be noted that this is not the same as preventing duplicative entries from being written into the mini-marts. The latter is taken care of in the load step.

As stated, a mini-mart is designed with easy data use in mind. The data must be user-centric and easily understandable. Coding the transform step should only start once sample data is available and has been checked and fully understood, and only after there is a clear specification-by-example of how the data will look in the mini-marts, identical to how the user sees the data. It might be tempting to skip these business-centric steps and address the mini-mart primarily from a technical perspective. You must not fall prey to this; always start with the question, "What does one row tell me in simple business terms?" Also have a screenshot ready of how a user sees "their data" in "their system," the system in which the data originates.

Using SQL for your ETL pipeline, as in the example below, helps test the transformation early. Check the content and correctness of the transformation early on before running any load. Run sanity and consistency checks. That is easily said and easily done. The *select* statement embedded in the transform step gives you the data in a user-friendly form even before creating the temporary table. Resist the temptation to haste. Move on to the load step only after checking for and correcting obvious data transformation errors. Before proceeding, perform a thorough pragmatic check of the content of the intermediary table with a subject-matter expert.

---

## Load

In this section, we update the mini-marts with minimal write operations that are robust to possible erroneous or duplicated input data.

The subsequent sections incrementally address the three complexity levels of loading the transformed data into the mini-marts.

1. Basic load: each record stands on its own and the mini-mart simply reflects the data's most recent content in the source systems.

2. Historization or Versioning: the content in the mini-marts reflects the change history as content-at-source changes.

3. Atomic lists: Lists of records with no clear unique identifier. Any entry in that list might be changed, deleted, or newly inserted, but the content of the mini-mart reflects the content of the list no matter the number and type of changes in between.

Before addressing these, let's briefly look at audit columns.

## Audit fields

In this section, we look at data traceability. Each entry in the mini-mart should have at least the following audit fields[37].

| | |
|---|---|
| mm_source_system | An identification of the technical source system from which the data was extracted. This is not necessarily the business source system, especially in cases in which data is provided by messaging middleware or has to be retrieved from an intermediary system. |
| mm_created_by | The process or job or any other suitable identifier to indicate who/what created that entry. |
| mm_created_timestamp | The timestamp of the first creation of this record. |
| mm_updated_by | The process or job or any other suitable identifier to indicate who/what updated that entry last. |
| mm_ updated _timestamp | The timestamp of the last update of this record. see details on versioning / type 2 tables |
| mm_delta_hash | A hash to identify whether any value on that record changed. |
| mm_current | Boolean. Enables smooth extension of any mini-mart to historicization and versioning or to data quality tagging without impacting existing usage. |

Figure 53: Generic audit columns

## Basic load

Basic load is simple: insert new, updated existing records and avoid erroneous duplication of already-existing entries.[38] Sample see further down.

## Historicization and versioning

In this section, we keep track of changes in dimensions and in facts.

---

[37] The column names are just suggestions for illustration. You can choose any naming convention; the important thing is to have a naming convention.

[38] See page with Sample Codes.

Historicization and versioning mean keeping track of changes in the same "entry." Sometimes the term "slowly changing dimensions" is used. Either a value changes and the mini-mart needs to track its changes, or not. While type 1 marts only retain the most recent values, type 2 marts keep track of changes. Columnar stores compress repeated values, making type 2 very efficient.

In type 2 marts, new data does not overwrite the existing data. Instead, we write a new version of the record into the mini-mart, and the old version is labeled accordingly. See "sample code."

Obviously, there is never a free lunch. Classical change control techniques readily identify the value changed yet need complex assembling to provide the complete record retrospectively for any point in time. The approach presented here requires comparing two records to identify which individual value changed. However, retrieving the complete record back in time is easy and fast.

We add the following additional columns to a mini-mart of type 2. Examples are in code samples.

| | |
|---|---|
| mm_version_number | A sequential number of the version. |
| mm_current | Boolean, true if this record is the most recent, current version, false otherwise. |
| mm_version_valid_from | The date/timestamp where this record became valid, where the source system started having the values as in this records version. |
| mm_version_valid_to | The date/timestamp just before this record changed again and became no longer valid. |

Figure 54: Additional audit columns for Type 2

## Loading atomic lists

In this section, we look at the typical challenge of replicating lists even in nasty real-life situations where no unique primary key is exposed.

We briefly discussed atomicity earlier concerning message-based integration. According to Wikipedia: "*In* database systems, *atomicity ... is one of the ACID (Atomicity, Consistency, Isolation, Durability) properties. An atomic transaction is an indivisible and irreducible series of database operations such that either all occurs, or nothing occurs. A guarantee of atomicity prevents updates to the database occurring only partially, which can cause greater problems than rejecting the whole series outright...*"[39]

We extend this definition to lists and define atomic lists as follows: "An atomic list is complete and irreducible and processed in its entirety." It is a good practice NOT to use internal technical

---

[39] https://en.wikipedia.org/wiki/ACID.

keys outside their source system. Using internal technical keys outside the intended system causes cross-dependencies limiting your freedom to act when upgrading or replacing systems.

Examples of an atomic list can be a list of names for a material, synonyms stored in a reference system, or key/value pairs. In SAP, these are called characteristics; in JSON structures, these are arrays. Sometimes, these lists have no unique key. The key is just the arbitrary sequence of the array in JSON or the unique key is hidden inside the source system and not exposed. Consequently, when seeing only one entry, one cannot know whether this is a new entry to be added to the list, a replacement of an existing entry, or the only entry of the list. Such lists can exist in dimensions like a list of many names for a material or in multi-layer facts.

A few criteria must be met to reliably replicate such lists in the mini-mart:

- Atomicity must be clearly defined; this is the scope of the list. This can be all key_values and all names for each individual material "in process" or all line-items for a Salesplan. Sometimes, this definition needs to be made explicit and sometimes it is implicit in the case of the entire array and nested arrays within a JSON.

- The source system must publish/send/expose the entire list. For example, it must contain all names for a material or the entire sub-array in JSON containing all entries, not just a subset thereof.

Loading atomic lists thus ensures that entries no longer existing are deleted or historized, and new entries are added. The mini-mart contains an exact copy while minimizing write operations even without unique keys.

---

# Sample code

In this section, we list sample codes to illustrate certain concepts. Ingestion from the source into the staging area is independent of the type of mini-mart but is very source-technology-specific. This section contains sample code for various complete transformation and load processes for different types of mini-marts in the example of AWS Redshift. We write for clarity and robustness, not necessarily for performance. The latter depends on the database technology chosen. The samples are in increasing order of complexity.

| Type of mini-mart | Focus of Sample Code |
|---|---|
| Simple mini-mart | o  denormalization and transformation<br>o  load while avoiding erroneous duplicates |
| Type 2 mini-mart historicization/versioning | o  adjusted load statement for historicization [transform step is unchanged] |
| Multi-layer facts | o  denormalization and transformation [load is unchanged] |
| Atomic Lists | o  adjusted load statement [transform step is unchanged] |

## Simple mini-mart

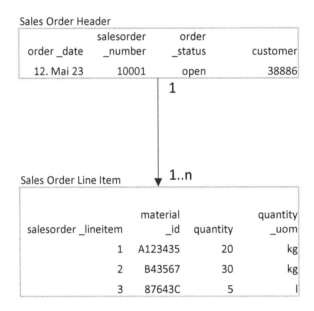

Figure 55: ER for the simplest example of join

First, we examine a transformation of the simplest sales order with order date, order status, customer, and a series of products sold.

There are only dimensions and qualifying attributes at the header level. Therefore, we can simply join the data.

### Transform

Creating the intermediary table. Some audit fields are omitted to keep the sample code shorter.

A few things should be noted:

1. fact_guid is a proxy for the unique key of any record. This makes the load statement independent of any specific business rules for the unique business key, even if multiple sources consolidated into the same mini-mart have different unique business keys.

2. The source system is made explicit and part of the fact_guid. This ensures that further source systems can be added at no risk even if they coincidentally have the same salesorder number and line item.

3. mm_delta_hash is calculated from all fields not part of the unique business key.

4. Lines 12 and 22 to 24: All md5's ensure that there is no erroneous <null>. The NVL function translates <null> into a defined value. The value '9999-01-01' has been chosen arbitrarily. Any valid value is good as it is only to create a valid md5 in the unlikely case of <null> and has no further meaning.

```
1    create temporary table tmp02_t_salesorder_fact ………..
2
3    insert
4        into
5        tmp02_t_salesorder_fact
6        (      fact_guid        , salesorder_number   , customer_id , order_date
7            , order_status , salesorder_lineitem , material_id , quantity
8            , quantity_uom
9            , mm_source_system , mm_delta_hash   )
10   select
11       distinct
12           md5('sapab' || (l.salesorder_number) || nvl(l.salesorder_lineitem, '-' ))
                                          as fact_guid
13       , h.salesorder_number        as salesorder_number
14       , h.customer                 as customer_id
15       , h.order_date               as order_date
16       , h.order_status             as order_status
17       , l.salesorder_lineitem      as salesorder_lineitem
18       , l.product                  as material_id
19       , l.quantity
20       , l.quantity_uom
21       , 'sapab'                    as mm_source_system
22       , md5(nvl(h.customer, '-')   || nvl(h.order_date, '9999-01-01')
23       || nvl(h.order_status, '-') || nvl(l.product, '-')
24       || nvl(l.quantity, 0)       || nvl(l.quantity_uom, '-') )
25                                    as mm_delta_hash
26   from spectrum.sapab_salesorder_header h
27   join spectrum.sapab_salesorder_lineitem l on  h.salesorder_number =
     l.salesorder_number
```

Sample Code 21: Basic Transform

## Basic load

Loading a simple type 1 mart has two steps: inserting new entries and updating existing ones.[40]

```
1    insert into mm03_t_salesorder_fact
2        (fact_guid
3        ,salesorder_number              ,salesorder_lineitem
4        ,customer_id
5        ,order_date                     ,order_status
6        ,material_id
7        ,quantity                       ,quantity_uom
8        ,mm_source_system
9        ,mm_delta_hash
10       ,mm_create_datetime             ,mm_update_datetime)
11       select
12           fact_guid
13           ,salesorder_number          ,salesorder_lineitem
14           ,customer_id
15           ,order_date                 ,order_status
16           ,material_id
17           ,quantity                   ,quantity_uom
18           ,mm_source_system
19           ,mm_delta_hash
20           ,getdate() as mm_create_datetime  ,getdate() as mm_update_datetime
21       from tmp02_t_salesorder_fact newdata
22       where newdata.fact_guid not in (select fact_guid from
     mm03_t_salesorder_fact)
23       ;
```

Sample Code 22: Basic Insert into Mini-Mart preventing Duplicates

Note:

- Only records are inserted whose fact_guid is not yet in the mini-mart [line 22]. This prevents erroneous duplicates. Depending on the database system, replacing the not exists by an outer join might be faster.

- Even fields forming the unique business key are included in the update statement although they never update. This is not necessary, but it makes the update statement very generic and free of any business knowledge or content, making the industrialization of ETL processes easier.

---

[40] Columns have been grouped on the same line for the sole purpose of reducing the number of lines to be shown on one page. There is no further meaning in this.

```
 1   update mm03_t_salesorder_fact
 2      set
 3            salesorder_number      =    newdata.salesorder_number
 4            ,customer_id           =    newdata.customer_id
 5            ,order_date            =    newdata.order_date
 6            ,order_status          =    newdata.order_status
 7            ,salesorder_lineitem   =    newdata.salesorder_lineitem
 8            ,material_id           =    newdata.material_id
 9            ,quantity              =    newdata.quantity
10            ,quantity_uom          =    newdata.quantity_uom
11            ,mm_source_system      =    newdata.mm_source_system
12            ,mm_delta_hash         =    newdata.mm_delta_hash
13            ,mm_update_datetime    =    getdate()
14      from tmp02_t_salesorder_fact newdata
15         where newdata.fact_guid = mm03_t_salesorder_fact.fact_guid
16            and newdata.mm_delta_hash <> mm03_t_salesorder_fact.mm_delta_hash
17   ;
```

Sample Code 23: Update of Changed Data Only

Note:

- Only records are updated that have a different mm_delta_hash for the same record identified by its fact_guid. This prevents unnecessary write operations in situations in which the same data is sent multiple times.

- mm_update_datetime is updated if there is changed data but not mm_create_datetime.

The resulting data appears below. Note the changed values for line item 2.

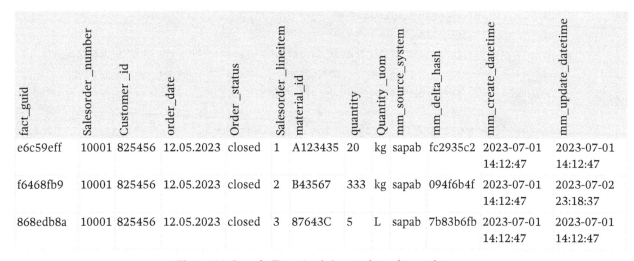

| fact_guid | Salesorder _number | Customer _id | order_date | Order _status | Salesorder _lineitem | material_id | quantity | Quantity _uom | mm_source _system | mm_delta_hash | mm_create _datetime | mm_update _datetime |
|---|---|---|---|---|---|---|---|---|---|---|---|---|
| e6c59eff | 10001 | 825456 | 12.05.2023 | closed | 1 | A123435 | 20 | kg | sapab | fc2935c2 | 2023-07-01 14:12:47 | 2023-07-01 14:12:47 |
| f6468fb9 | 10001 | 825456 | 12.05.2023 | closed | 2 | B43567 | 333 | kg | sapab | 094f6b4f | 2023-07-01 14:12:47 | 2023-07-02 23:18:37 |
| 868edb8a | 10001 | 825456 | 12.05.2023 | closed | 3 | 87643C | 5 | L | sapab | 7b83b6fb | 2023-07-01 14:12:47 | 2023-07-01 14:12:47 |

Figure 56: Sample Type 1 mini-mart data after update

## Type 2, historicization

### Load

There are three steps involved for type 2 data loads: insert genuinely new entries, insert changed entries, and tag entries that became obsolete. Only the load step is different between type 1 mini-marts with current data only and type 2 mini-marts performing historicization. The ingestion and transform steps are unchanged.

Step 1: Inserting new data. Note the change between lines 23 and 24 versus type 1 mini-marts.

```
1    insert into mm03_t_salesorder_fact
2         (fact_guid
3         ,salesorder_number               ,salesorder_lineitem
4         ,customer_id
5         ,order_date                      ,order_status
6         ,material_id
7         ,quantity                        ,quantity_uom
8         ,mm_source_system
9         ,mm_delta_hash
10        ,mm_create_datetime   ,mm_update_datetime
11        ,mm_version_number ,mm_version_current
12        ,mm_version_valid_from ,mm_version_valid_to )
13        select
14            fact_guid
15            ,salesorder_number             ,salesorder_lineitem
16            ,customer_id
17            ,order_date                    ,order_status
18            ,material_id
19            ,quantity                      ,quantity_uom
20            ,mm_source_system
21            ,mm_delta_hash
22            ,getdate() as mm_create_datetime   ,getdate() as mm_update_datetime
23            ,1          as mm_version_number   ,true      as mm_version_current
24            ,getdate() as mm_version_valid_from    ,'9999-12-31' as mm_version_valid_to
25        from tmp03_t_salesorder_fact newdata
26        where newdata.fact_guid not in (select fact_guid from mm03_t_salesorder_fact)
27        ;
```

Sample Code 24: Load, Insert New Entries For Type 2

It can be seen that line 24 might not be elegant, but it is pragmatic. Avoid <null> in *mm_version_valid_to*. If this date is set for the current record to eternity [i.e., 9999-12-31], then the statement

*"where <date> is between mm_version_valid_from_and mm_version_valid_to"*

will always return a valid result. Otherwise, it might evaluate to <null> and not return any records or every user must explicitly code for <null> in *mm_version_valid_to*.

Step 2: Insert the changed data. Note the version number increase in line 26 and preservation of the original create_datetime in 24 while setting the update timestamp for this version of the data in line 25.

```
1    insert into mm03_t_salesorder_fact
2        (fact_guid
3        ,salesorder_number                   ,salesorder_lineitem
4        ,customer_id
5        ,order_date                          ,order_status
6        ,material_id
7        ,quantity                            ,quantity_uom
8        ,mm_source_system
9        ,mm_delta_hash
10       ,mm_create_datetime
11       ,mm_update_datetime
12       ,mm_version_number
13       ,mm_version_current
14       ,mm_version_valid_from               ,mm_version_valid_to )
15       select
16           newdata.fact_guid
17           ,newdata.salesorder_number       ,newdata.salesorder_lineitem
18           ,newdata.customer_id
19           ,newdata.order_date              ,newdata.order_status
20           ,newdata.material_id
21           ,newdata.quantity                ,newdata.quantity_uom
22           ,newdata.mm_source_system
23           ,newdata.mm_delta_hash
24           ,exisdata.mm_create_datetime       as mm_create_datetime
25           ,getdate()                         as mm_update_datetime
26           ,exisdata.mm_version_number + 1    as mm_version_number
27           ,true
28           ,newdata.mm_version_valid_from   ,newdata.mm_version_valid_to
29         from tmp03_t_salesorder_fact                newdata
30         join mm03_t_salesorder_fact  exisdata
31              on exisdata.fact_guid = newdata.fact_guid
                    and exisdata.mm_version_current
32        where newdata.mm_delta_hash <> exisdata.mm_delta_hash
33    ;
```

Sample Code 25: Load type- 2 insert changed data

Step 3: Update obsolete version. Note the use of mm_delta_hash. This ensures that only the older version is updated.

```
1     update mm03_t_salesorder_fact
2         set
3             mm_version_valid_to    =   newdata.mm_version_valid_from - 1
4             ,mm_version_current    =   false
5         from mm03_t_salesorder_fact  exisdata  -- identify existing record having an update
6         join tmp02_t_salesorder_fact                  newdata
7             on  exisdata.fact_guid = newdata.fact_guid
8             and exisdata.mm_version_current
9             and newdata.mm_delta_hash <> exisdata.mm_delta_hash
10        where mm03_t_salesorder_fact.fact_guid = exisdata.fact_guid
11          and mm03_t_salesorder_fact.mm_version_current
```

Sample Code 26: Load type 2 update previous version

Note line 3. Set this date or datetime to one day or millisecond below the *mm_version_valid_from* of the new record. In this way, a simple *between mm_version_valid_from and mm_version_valid_to* always return exactly one record only. It could return two records, an old and a new version, if valid_to of the previous version is identical to valid_from of the new version. The resulting data contains the change history. Each line item has exactly one entry with *mm_version_current* = true. Older entries for this line-item have *mm_version_current* = false and the historical validity date in version valid from / valid to. The quantity of line-item 2 and 3 have changed, one of them twice. Some values were only valid for one day.

| salesorder_number | customer_id | order_date | order_status | salesorder_lineitem | material_id | quantity | quantity_uom | mm_source_system | mm_delta_hash | mm_create_datetime | mm_update_datetime | mm_version_number | mm_version_current | mm_version_valid_from | mm_version_valid_to |
|---|---|---|---|---|---|---|---|---|---|---|---|---|---|---|---|
| 10001 | 38886 | 2022.05.12 | closed | 1 | A123435 | 20 | kg | sapab | fc2935c2 | 2022-07-05 | 2022-07-05 | 1 | TRUE | 2022.07.05 | 9999.12.31 |
| 10001 | 38886 | 2022.05.12 | closed | 2 | B43567 | 333 | kg | sapab | 094f6b4f | 2022-07-05 | 2022-07-05 | 1 | false | 2022.07.05 | 2022.07.05 |
| 10001 | 38886 | 2022.05.12 | closed | 2 | B43567 | 33 | kg | sapab | 0f6724b6 | 2022-07-05 | 2022-07-06 | 2 | false | 2022.07.06 | 2022.07.06 |
| 10001 | 38886 | 2022.05.12 | closed | 2 | B43567 | 3 | kg | sapab | 7f2a4dd8 | 2022-07-05 | 2022-07-07 | 3 | TRUE | 2022.07.07 | 9999.12.31 |
| 10001 | 38886 | 2022.05.12 | closed | 3 | 87643C | 55 | L | sapab | 04975e2e | 2022-07-05 | 2022-07-05 | 1 | false | 2022.07.05 | 2022.07.06 |
| 10001 | 38886 | 2022.05.12 | closed | 3 | 87643C | 5 | L | sapab | 7b83b6fb | 2022-07-05 | 2022-07-07 | 2 | TRUE | 2022.07.07 | 9999.12.31 |

Figure 57: Sample Type 2 data

Historicization is free of business assumptions. Changing a mini-mart from type 1 to type 2 needs no business knowledge and can be fully industrialized. It only requires changing the load steps. This can be done even after the mini-mart has first been implemented as type 1 and later upgraded to type 2. The transformation itself does not need to be changed.

## Transforming multi-layer facts

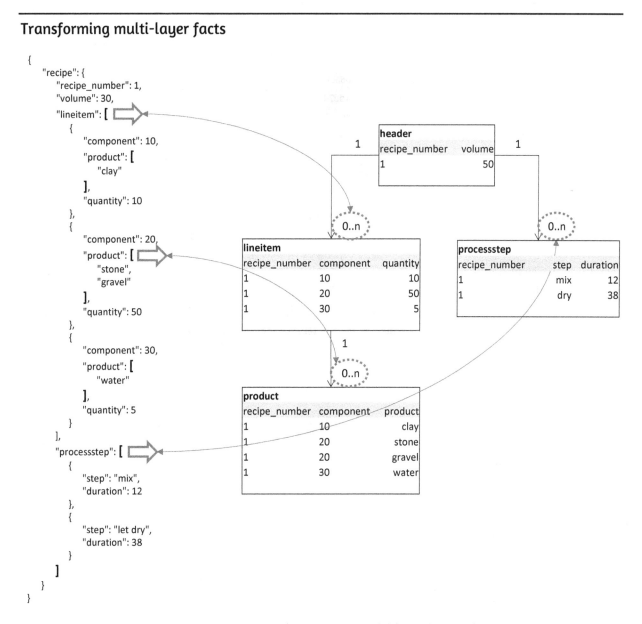

Figure 58: Mapping JSON of recipe to ER model for multi-layer facts

The transformation of multi-layer facts appears in the example of the recipe with the alternate products shown earlier.

This example has measures at almost every level except at the product level. These measures are volume, quantity, and duration. It has a few classifying columns, such as recipe_number, component, product, and step.

| l0_guid | l1_guid | l2_guid | mm_record _level | record_type | fact_guid | recipe _number | volume | componen t | quantity | product | step | duration |
|---|---|---|---|---|---|---|---|---|---|---|---|---|
| ca423 | | | 0 | header | ca423 | 1 | 50 | | | | | |
| ca423 | 93f98 | | 1 | lineitem | 93f98 | 1 | | 10 | 10 | | | |
| ca423 | 93f98 | 7e6c0 | 2 | product | 7e6c0 | 1 | | 10 | | clay | | |
| ca423 | 86192 | | 1 | lineitem | 86192 | 1 | | 30 | 5 | | | |
| ca423 | 86192 | f28bc | 2 | product | f28bc | 1 | | 30 | | water | | |
| ca423 | 4fb5c | | 1 | lineitem | 4fb5c | 1 | | 20 | 50 | | | |
| ca423 | 4fb5c | c8a2f | 2 | product | c8a2f | 1 | | 20 | | gravel | | |
| ca423 | 4fb5c | 4dc74 | 2 | product | 4dc74 | 1 | | 20 | | stone | | |
| ca423 | ce7d1 | | 1 | processstep | ce7d1 | 1 | | | | | mix | 12 |
| ca423 | 93cd6 | | 1 | processstep | 93cd6 | 1 | | | | | dry | 38 |

Figure 59: Sample multi-layer facts

The ETL process for multi-layer facts is not substantially changed compared to normal, flat, one-level fact mini-marts. The process first creates an intermediary table that is then used in a basic load, for updating atomic lists and versioning data when needed.

Transforming each record type individually is the most transparent and easiest to maintain. It is used in the following example. This eliminates the complexities of aligning long lists of column names in union statements. Using individual inserts into the intermediary table is less prone to coding errors and the mini-mart is easier to extend if additional columns are required.

The coding blueprint repeats for each level for which this multi-layer fact has a measure. Levels without a measure are just logical levels and do not need a dedicated record_type.

- Attributes forming the business key, even implicit, are contributing to GUIDs
  When loading the intermediary table into the mini-mart, the atomic list's ambiguity is addressed.

- All other columns are contributing to mm_delta_hash

- Handle <null> values so they return a valid delta_hash nevertheless.

- Dimensions and classifying attributes are repeated at every level, while measures are exclusively at the level of the relevant record.

```
1    insert into tmp02_t_recipe_fact
2    (record_type, mm_record_level, fact_guid, l0_guid, recipe_number, volume,
     mm_delta_hash)
3    select
4       'header'                                  as record_type
5       ,0                                        as mm_record_level
6       ,md5(h.recipe_number) as fact_guid
7       ,md5(h.recipe_number) as l0_guid
8       ,h.recipe_number
9       ,h.volume
10      ,md5(nvl(h.volume,0))    as mm_delta_hash
11      from spectrum.header          h
12      ;
```

Sample Code 27: Multi-layer facts, insert header (L0) into intermediary table

Insert header records into the intermediary table.

```
1    insert into tmp02_t_recipe_fact
2    (record_type, mm_record_level, fact_guid, l0_guid, l1_guid, recipe_number,
     component , quantity, mm_delta_hash )
3    select
4       'lineitem'  as record_type
5       ,1                                          as mm_record_level
6       ,md5(h.recipe_number || nvl(l.component,'-' ))   as fact_guid
7       ,md5(h.recipe_number)                            as l0_guid
8       ,md5(h.recipe_number || nvl(l.component,'-' ))   as l1_guid
9       ,h.recipe_number
10      ,l.component, l.quantity
11      ,md5(nvl(l.quantity,0))   as mm_delta_hash
12    from spectrum.header          h
13    join spectrum.lineitem        l on h.recipe_number = l.recipe_number
14    ;
```

Sample Code 28: Multi-layer facts, insert line item (L1) into intermediary table

Insert line items. Note that l0_guid is calculated by the same rule as for headers. This ensures correct internal references between the various record_types.

Insert the product alternatives into the intermediary table.

```
1   insert into tmp02_t_recipe_fact
2   (record_type, mm_record_level, fact_guid, l0_guid, l1_guid, l2_guid
    , recipe_number, component, product, mm_delta_hash )
3   select
4         'product'  as record_type
5         ,2          as mm_record_level
6         ,md5(l.recipe_number || nvl(l.component,'-' ) || nvl(p.product,'-' ))
                                                      as fact_guid
7         ,md5(h.recipe_number)                       as l0_guid
8         ,md5(h.recipe_number || nvl(l.component,'-' ))      as l1_guid
9         ,md5(l.recipe_number || nvl(l.component,'-' ) || nvl(p.product,'-' ))
                                                      as l2_guid
10        ,h.recipe_number
11        ,l.component
12        ,p.product
13        ,md5(0)     as mm_delta_hash
14    from spectrum.header        h
15    join spectrum.lineitem      l on h.recipe_number = l.recipe_number
16    join spectrum.product       p on l.recipe_number = p.recipe_number
17                                    and l.component = p.component      ;
```

Sample Code 29: Multi-layer facts, insert alternate products (L2) into intermediary table

Insert the process steps.

```
1   insert into tmp02_t_recipe_fact
2   (record_type, mm_record_level, fact_guid, l0_guid, l1_guid
    , recipe_number, step, duration , mm_delta_hash)
3   select
4         'processstep'  as record_type
5         ,1                              as mm_record_level
6         ,md5(h.recipe_number || nvl(s.step,'-' )) as fact_guid
7         ,md5(h.recipe_number)           as l0_guid
8         ,md5(h.recipe_number || nvl(s.step,'-' )) as l1_guid
9         ,h.recipe_number
10        ,s.step   , s.duration
11        ,md5(nvl(s.duration,0))   as mm_delta_hash
12    from spectrum.header        h
13    join spectrum.processstep   s on h.recipe_number = s.recipe_number
14    ;
```

Sample Code 30: Multi-layer facts, insert process steps (L1) into intermediary table

The intermediary table resulting from the steps above can then be loaded into the mini-mart. This way, we ensure that entries no longer existing in new recipe versions are removed and others updated. This is done using the concept of atomic lists.

## Atomic lists

To recap from the foregoing, atomic lists ensure that entire lists of entries with no unique key are correctly replicated, irrespective of whether there are changes, inserts, or deletions. The ingestion and transformation steps are identical to any other type of mini-mart. Only the load step must be adapted to cope correctly with atomic lists.

Atomic lists do not make any assumptions about unique keys. This is useful in cases where internal unique keys are not exposed by the source system and for replicating complex JSON structures with arrays. As stated before, we should never expose the internal key of any system outside or used beyond the originating system.

Loading atomic lists first and foremost requires clarity about the scope of the atomicity. A clear definition of the data belonging together is needed, a list of data that is an inseparable unit. Examples of atomicity can be:

- All product names for a given material from a given source.

- All product names for a given material irrespective of its source system.

- As in the previous JSON example, an entire recipe with all its dependent objects, line items, alternate products, and process steps.

- All of the properties for a specification such as length, height, weight, color, etc.

- All names/terms for an object.

Loading an atomic list has two steps:

1. Delete orphans, entries not contained in the new list.

2. Insert new entries – and leave entries already existing unchanged.

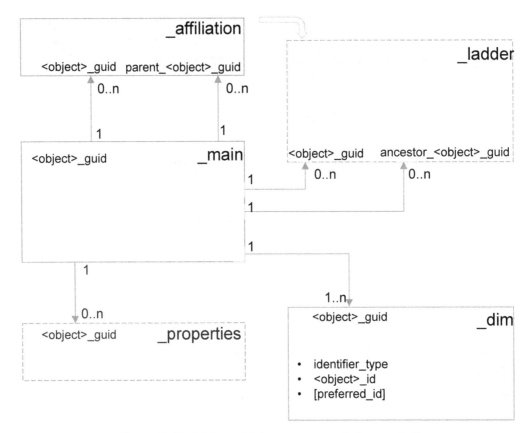

Figure 60: Model for multiple terms, example for atomic list

**Sample list**

Our first example uses material properties.

Let's quickly review the model for a dimension we used earlier. There is a _main with one entry per object, the _IDs in _Dim, and often a few dependent multiple objects like terms or names, key/value pairs, or material properties. It is a judgment call whether these properties are actually part of the dimensional mini-mart or (factless) facts in their own right. I personally see it as pragmatic. If these data points inherently belong to the dimension, are a key property of any entry in _main, are seen by the data users as inherently part of the dimension, and are not created by continuous transactions using the dimension, then I add them to the dimension's mini-mart. We use the example below only to illustrate the concept of atomic lists.

We have cars with properties. Here is the original list:

| material_number | description | property_name | property_value |
|---|---|---|---|
| 1 | car | color | white |
| | | | blue |
| | | weight | 2222 |
| 2 | truck | color | green |
| | | weight | 7777 |

Later, the data changes. Cars come in white and orange and trucks also come in black.

| material_number | description | property_name | property_value |
|---|---|---|---|
| 1 | car | color | white |
| | | | orange |
| | | weight | 2222 |
| 2 | truck | color | green |
| | | | black |
| | | weight | 7777 |

```
1   insert into tmp04_t_material_property
2   (material_guid, mm_source_system, property_name, property_value, mm_delta_hash)
3   select
4         d.material_guid
5         ,'sapab'                 as mm_source_system
6         ,property_name           as property_name
7         ,property_value          as property_value
8         ,md5(nvl(property_name,'-') || nvl(property_value,'-') ) as mm_delta_hash
9      from spectrum.sapab_property        1
10     join mm04_t_material_dim d on 1.material_number = d.material_id
11        ;
```

Sample Code 31: Atomic list transformation step example

The transform step is unchanged from any other transformation. Note that the GUID is derived in line 10 from _dim. This enables consolidating information from different source systems for the same material. These source systems can contribute properties to the same material regardless of the material's synonym used by any particular source system.

The atomicity of the data in this example is defined as "a complete list of properties for any given material from the source system SAPAB."

The delete steps must remove all properties not existing in the new list for each material and not contained in the new set of properties. The insert step inserts new entries only, thereby reducing the number of write operations while being completely agnostic to the data, whether any data was sent twice, and which entries changed at all.

Deleting orphans from the mini-mart:

```
1    delete
3        from mm04_t_material_property
4        where material_guid    in (select material_guid from tmp04_t_material_property)
5          and mm_source_system in ( 'sapab' )
6          and not exists        (
7                 select newlist.material_guid
8                     from tmp04_t_material_property newlist
9                     where newlist.material_guid    = mm04_t_material_property.material_guid
10                      and newlist.mm_delta_hash    = mm04_t_material_property.mm_delta_hash
11                )
```

Sample Code 32: Atomic list delete orphans example

Note:

- Lines 4 and 5 define the atomicity, delete only materials contained in the new data and only those from the source system SAPAB.

- Lines 6 to 10, delete only the rows identified by delta_hash that are NOT contained in the new set of properties for a material. The sample data above will remove the entry for the color blue.

The next step is inserting new data into the mini-mart.

```
1    insert into mm04_t_material_property
2        (material_guid, mm_source_system, property_name, property_value,
     mm_delta_hash, mm_create_datetime, mm_update_datetime  )
3    select
4        material_guid
5        , mm_source_system
6        , property_name
7        , property_value
8        , mm_delta_hash
9        , getdate()
10       , getdate()
11       from  tmp04_t_material_property newlist
12       where not exists
13          ( select material_guid  from mm04_t_material_property existlist
14              where  newlist.mm_delta_hash = existlist.mm_delta_hash
15                and  newlist.material_guid = existlist.material_guid
16          )
17    ;
```

Sample Code 33: Atomic list insert new entries example

Note lines 12 to 15; they make sure only rows get inserted for new entries, not those already existing with the same guid and delta_hash[41]. The resulting data appears in the following table.

| material_id | business_unit | material_guid | property_name | property_value | mm_source_system | mm_delta_hash | mm_create_datetime |
|---|---|---|---|---|---|---|---|
| 1 | car | c4ca4238a0 | color | white | sapab | 18214f742b3 | 2023-07-05 15:27:56.000 |
| | | | color | orange | sapab | 10dfb41ea58 | 2023-07-06 17:36:45.000 |
| | | | weight | 2222 | sapab | a2304818bd8 | 2023-07-05 15:27:56.000 |
| 2 | truck | c81e728d9d | color | green | sapab | c9e6f36675b9 | 2023-07-05 15:36:38.000 |
| | | | color | black | sapab | c54c668b32e8 | 2023-07-06 17:36:45.000 |
| | | | weight | 7777 | sapab | 59ade837170a | 2023-07-05 15:27:56.000 |

Figure 61: Sample data for an atomic list

Note the difference in the mm_create_datetime columns. Some entries were inserted at half past three while others were inserted one day and two hours later. The blue entry was removed for cars, orange added, and black was added to trucks.

The above logic does not make any assumptions about the data constellation other than that data is complete for any given material from a source system. Only the transformation step needs business and application knowledge to transform the data; all other steps are fully generic and can be industrialized.

**Example of multi-layer facts**

In the next example, we upsert[42] the recipe information. The JSON on which the recipe is based has no information about whether or which entries have been added or removed since the last time this recipe was sent. The source system should not publish any internal keys for individual entries in the recipe and we do not want to make any assumptions about the data.

---

[41] Again, the example is for clarity. Replacing the not exists by an outer join might be faster, depending on the DBMS used.

[42] Upsert: insert if not existing, update if already existing.

Atomicity is our only business information. The data for any recipe is complete. This atomicity is defined by the l0_guid. Furthermore, the generic rules for transformation define fact_guid and delta_hash as joint surrogate information for a unique record.

The steps remain the same, delete orphans and insert new entries.

Deleting orphan entries

```
1    delete
2        from mm02_t_recipe_fact
3        where    L0_guid in
4            (select L0_guid from tmp02_t_recipe_fact)
5          and not exists          (
6                select newlist.L0_guid
7                    from tmp02_t_recipe_fact newlist
8                    where newlist.L0_guid          = mm02_t_recipe_fact.L0_guid
9                        and newlist.fact_guid          = mm02_t_recipe_fact.fact_guid
10                       and newlist.mm_delta_hash    = mm02_t_recipe_fact.mm_delta_hash
11            )
12  ;
```

Sample Code 34: Atomic list delete orphans on example of JSON recipe

Lines 3 and 4 ensure that only recipes contained in the new data are even candidates for orphan deletion while lines 8 to 10 identify those entries not existing anymore in the new data.

## Inserting new entries

```
1    insert into mm02_t_recipe_fact
2        (l0_guid        ,l1_guid        ,l2_guid
3        ,mm_record_level
4        ,record_type
5        ,fact_guid
6        ,recipe_number
7        ,volume
8        ,component
9        ,quantity
10       ,product
11       ,step
12       ,duration
13       ,mm_delta_hash
14       ,mm_create_datetime
15       ,mm_update_datetime)
16       select
17           l0_guid        ,l1_guid        ,l2_guid
18           ,mm_record_level
19           ,record_type
20           ,fact_guid
21           ,recipe_number
22           ,volume
23           ,component
24           ,quantity
25           ,product
26           ,step
27           ,duration
28           ,mm_delta_hash
29           ,getdate() as mm_create_datetime
30           ,getdate() as mm_update_datetime
31       from tmp02_t_recipe_fact newlist
32       where not exists
33           ( select L0_guid  from mm02_t_recipe_fact existlist
34             where  newlist.fact_guid       = existlist.fact_guid
35               and  newlist.mm_delta_hash   = existlist.mm_delta_hash
36               and  newlist.L0_guid         = existlist.L0_guid
37           )
38   ;
```

Sample Code 35: Atomic list insert new entries for recipe example

Further optimizations are possible.

- Replace "not exists" by a *join* statement.

- If *fact_guid* is a guaranteed surrogate key for any entry, then deletion and insert can be based on l0_guid and *fact_guid* only and an update statement based on *delta_hash* can be added, potentially reducing the number of write operations.

- If type 2 is needed, then deletion can be replaced by updating *valid_to* date and *mm_current*.

A list can only be replicated correctly in any mini-mart if the source system guarantees the atomicity of the list. Otherwise, we cannot determine whether an isolated entry is a new entry, an update of an existing one, or the solitary entry only. Using internal technical keys from source systems in the mini-marts creates complex technical dependencies. Instead, update the mini-mart without making any assumptions about the data other than that the data for one "atomic entity" is complete. Achieve this by deleting orphans and inserting new entries. This applies to lists of dependent entries like multiple names for a dimension and multi-layer facts.

## Extending mini-marts

In this section, we look at how to adapt mini-marts to changing business requirements without impacting business continuity. Any enterprise data warehouse or lakehouse is never complete, or, as the saying goes, the appetite comes with the eating. Additional columns might be needed, the mini-mart needs historicization, additional sources are added, contributing to the same mini-mart. Extending an enterprise data warehouse of sufficient complexity means either creating parallel structures of similar content or open-heart surgery on the data lakehouse. The latter is costly and risky, so we often choose the former. It might result over time in multiple marts and cubes of similar content but with slightly different KPI definitions, data scope, or aggregations. The techniques used in the mini-marts mitigate parallel structures and open-heart surgery. Additional flows can be implemented independently of existing flows into the same mini-marts.

Mini-marts can be extended easily provided all implicit assumptions about data are made explicit and there are no physical limits like data locks. Implicit assumptions include an indication of source and classifying attributes qualifying the data subtype. Run an impact assessment to determine whether existing usages of the mart are explicitly filtering for source or classifying attributes. To extend a mini-mart, map the columns of the new source onto the business meaning of the existing columns, add additional columns if needed and implement the additional flow as any other flow is implemented. Regarding the mapping of columns to business meaning, I have seen cases in which *sales_price_min* from one source system and *sales_price_minimum* from another were two different columns in the same mini-mart. They can be consolidated into a joint column, *sales_price_minimum*, making data usage much easier. As stated above, the fact that not all sources can populate all columns of a mini-mart is not a sufficient reason for splitting the marts.

# EIGHT

# Using the Mini-Marts

This chapter explores the use of the enterprise data lakehouse we built in the previous chapters and highlights certain aspects of specific use cases. We saw in the introduction that we initiate mini-marts by specific business needs but are implemented in a generic way. This makes them reusable beyond the initial use case. The rules and techniques for such a generic implementation were described in the previous chapters, starting with the "Ask" for data-informed decision-making and continuing with the various blueprints for synonyms, flexible hierarchies, facts, multi-layer facts, and atomic lists. This chapter closes the loop by illustrating techniques on how to combine these mini-marts for analysis and inject specific business rules to address very specific business questions.

First, let's look at the usage patterns from the various levels of self-service to dashboarding to data science and machine learning. After that, we will address generic usage patterns, tips, and tricks for using the mini-marts that apply to the above usage patterns. We end the chapter with the various levels of usage simplification we can carry out, depending on the enterprise's requirements and degree of standardization. The technical aspects of using the mini-marts are independent of whether it is implemented as a data mesh, provided that cross-node access is possible and efficient.

## Self-service

There are various degrees of self-service, from using filtering on predefined reports to data guru.

| | My filter / My Visualization | No-code Self Service | Create my own Report | Data Guru |
|---|---|---|---|---|
| Audience | Routine operational reporting. Individual filters and personalized visualizations | Data-savvy business users familiar with business data but not SQL | Data-savvy business functions familiar with business data but not SQL | Developers, Data Gurus, and Data Science Professionals |
| Purpose | Answer repeating questions | Answer innovative questions | Answer innovative questions with appealing visualizations | Anything goes |
| Provided to user | Predefined dashboards | Access to the Mini-Marts at various levels of predefined simplifications | Access to the Mini-Marts at various levels of predefined simplifications | Access to the Mini-Marts at various levels |
| Primary Tool | Classical dashboarding tools | Scalable data-oriented self-service tools, e.g. Sigma Computing | Classical dashboarding tools claiming self-service capabilities at scale | Anything goes |
| Degree of Self | Change filter Adapt visualizations | Filter, aggregate and combine data, asking innovative questions | Combine data in novel ways, ask innovative questions and limited scale-up | Anything goes |

Figure 62: Degrees of self service

All users, except for the most basic ones, will use the mini-marts with some of the capabilities described for combining data and will use any of the usage simplifications. However, the usage pattern is different. No-code self-service tends to access the underlying mini-marts frequently for specific questions and rather smaller data volumes. This contrasts with in-memory dashboarding and training data for machine learning which require large data volumes but less frequently.

## Dashboarding

Modern dashboards complement real-time queries with pre-loaded data in memory. The latter provides users with substantially faster reaction times. Dashboarding, or more precisely creating dashboards, has the same basic requirements with respect to the data lakehouse as any other usage, yet the data volume for pre-loading in-memory data can be substantial. This requires OLAP models and might affect the technical platform for the data lakehouse.

More importantly, high data volumes require data aggregation in the backend, the data lakehouse. While it is entirely feasible to load a few million records efficiently into an in-memory dashboarding tool, it becomes challenging at larger volumes. Mini-marts might have a few hundred million, if not a few billion entries. Such data volumes require pre-aggregation and filtering of the data at the lakehouse level before being loaded into the dashboard. Generating those queries at the database level often requires some degree of coding, even though the tool might be promoted as needing just drag-and-drop.

## Common dimensions and synonyms

Next, let's look at robustness and simplicity even in the presence of multiple competing identifiers. We refer to our model enterprise using different identifiers for the same object. Examples are the different identifiers for the same material or the different identifiers for the same customer in the examples used. There might be unwritten rules, conventions, habits, and exceptions for when to use what or what is used where. Our enterprise data lakehouse, or more specifically, the usage thereof, must not depend on this fractional knowledge. It must be resilient to whatever identifier is used in a specific context. This is the whole reason why our design embraces synonyms from the very beginning. Look closely at the data below.

This example combines one fact table [sales order] with one common dimension [customer_id]. It is the most basic join between mini-marts.

```
1    select
2            c.customer_id
3            ,c.identifier_type
4            ,c.last_name
5            ,c.all_the_other_columns
6            ,s.salesorder_number
7            ,s.order_date
8            ,s.order_status
9            ,s.material_id
10           ,s.quantity
11           ,s.quantity_uom
12           ,s.mm_version_number
13           ,s.mm_version_current
14           ,s.mm_version_valid_from,s.mm_version_valid_to
15      from mm03_salesorder_fact s
16      join mm01_customer        c on c.customer_id = s.customer_id
```

Sample Code 36: Basic join between two Mini-Marts

We can see in the above example that the join in line 16 on customer_id is regardless of the identifier_type and synonym. We use the mm03_salesorder_fact view, which retrieves only the most recent values of a type 2 table. The example in Figure 63 relates to our model enterprise's fragmented customer data. We correctly join the customer data regardless of whether this customer is defined in the mdm system or in the sapxy and/or SAPAB system, even if the same customer has sales data from multiple systems using different identifiers [Seramis].

| customer_id | identifier_ type | last_name | Salesorder _number | order_date | order_ status | material_id | quantity quantity_uom |
|---|---|---|---|---|---|---|---|
| 38886 | mdm sapxy | Cruiser | 10007 | 2023-07-01 | open | B43567 | 1 kg |
| 825456 | mdm | Dicuran | 10001 | 2023-05-12 | closed | A123435 | 20 kg |
| 825456 | mdm | Dicuran | 10001 | 2023-05-12 | closed | B43567 | 3 kg |
| 825456 | mdm | Dicuran | 10001 | 2023-05-12 | closed | 87643C | 5 L |
| 140188 | sapab | Racumin | 20017 | 2023-07-22 | open | B43567 | 22 kg |
| 4043413 | sapab | Seramis | 20005 | 2023-05-08 | closed | 87643C | 11 kg |
| 02825dc45581 | rcp | Seramis | 600006 | 2023-06-22 | closed | A123435 | 111 kg |
| 107926 | sapab | Xerotin | 20015 | 2023-03-22 | closed | A123435 | 44 kg |

Figure 63: Sample data from different sales systems combined

## Using hierarchies

In this section, we will retrieve data from unbalanced, dynamic, and heterogenous hierarchies.

We reviewed hierarchies in the chapter about dimensions and explained _affiliation and _ladder. These constructs can accommodate many different hierarchies and qualify them with affiliation_type. In this section, we focus on the use of dynamic hierarchies. The following examples illustrate this on a small scale. We can easily extrapolate to large-scale organizations and picture the elegance and ease of flexibly adjusting hierarchies and query the impact thereof. Figure 64 shows the setup of the example.

This example builds on the customer hierarchies used earlier. The approach works as easily with sales_territory hierarchies or any other hierarchy.

Here we want all salesorders for all customers belonging to Seramis from a legal viewpoint. Note that this is a blueprint, querying data in flexible hierarchies. We will repeat the same hierarchy for your convenience.

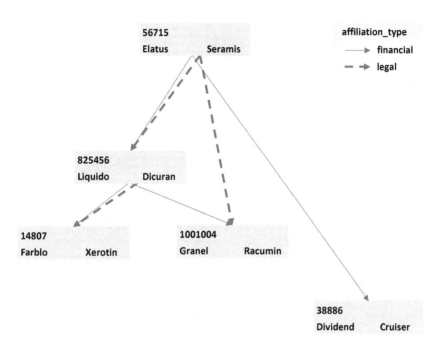

Figure 64: Sample customer hierarchy

The query is again optimized for clarity, not for performance.

```
1   select
2         c.customer_id
3         ,c.identifier_type
4         ,c.last_name
5         ,s.salesorder_number
6         ,s.order_date
7         ,s.material_id
8         ,s.quantity
9         ,s.quantity_uom
10    from mm03_salesorder_fact    s
11    join mm01_customer           c on c.customer_id = s.customer_id
12    where c.customer_guid in
13        (
14            select l.customer_guid
15                from mm01_customer_ladder l
16                join mm01_customer          c
17                    on c.customer_guid = l.ancestor_customer_guid
18                where c.last_name = 'Seramis'
19                  and l.affiliation_type = 'legal'
20        )
21        ;
```

Sample Code 37: Query infinite hierarchy

| customer_id | Identifier_type | last_name | Salesorder_number | order_date | material_id | quantity quantity_uom |
|---|---|---|---|---|---|---|
| 825456 | mdm | Dicuran | 10001 | 2023-05-12 | 87643C | 5 L |
| 825456 | mdm | Dicuran | 10001 | 2023-05-12 | B43567 | 3 kg |
| 825456 | mdm | Dicuran | 10001 | 2023-05-12 | A123435 | 20 kg |
| 140188 | sapab | Racumin | 20017 | 2023-07-22 | B43567 | 22 kg |
| 4043413 | sapab | Seramis | 20005 | 2023-05-08 | 87643C | 11 kg |
| 02825dc45581 | rcp | Seramis | 600006 | 2023-06-22 | A123435 | 111 kg |
| 107926 | sapab | Xerotin | 20015 | 2023-03-22 | A123435 | 44 kg |

Figure 65: Sample customer data from querying the hierarchy

Note that sales for Cruiser are not included. Cruiser is a financial yet not a legal dependent of Seramis. Cruiser would be included if we had selected for the financial relationship. All other entries are included irrespective of the depth of the hierarchy. Note also that customers are reported irrespective of their various customer_ids in the various source systems. Sales for Seramis are returned irrespective of the customer_id used in the respective sales systems.

# Affiliation and proximity

In this section, we showcase analysis using geographic proximity at scale.

Affiliations capture the "one-level" relationship between entries in a dimension such as organizational hierarchies. However, there is another use case for dimensions and affiliations: geographic proximity.

Let's assume weather statistics are available in a regular grid or from specific locations. There are also trials and farming activities carried out at specific locations. These must be correlated. There are elegant solutions available if the underlying DBMS supports spatial queries. In any case, correlating that geographic data and finding the closest weather station out of many may be computationally intensive, especially if training for machine learning requires large data sets.

In the section on generalization, we saw that any type of place is a place, whether it is a place for a weather station, a grid-point for a weather grid, or a location of a field or city. Any type of place can be affiliated with another one. A place of the trial location type can be related or affiliated with the closest place of the weather grid type. Generalizing all types of locations/places, and pre-calculating and persisting geographic proximity offers another approach for scalable location-based analysis even for large data volumes needed for training machine learning models.

This affiliation can be persisted in place_affiliation. It enables queries like the following:

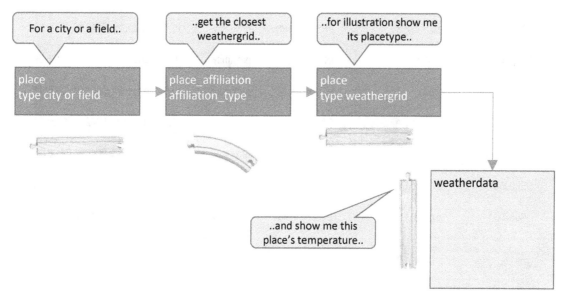

Figure 66: Data journey for weather data

```
1   select
2           p.place_id
3           , p.city_name , p.country_code  , p.place_type
4           , a.place_affiliation_type , a.distance_km
5           , c.place_id
6           , c.place_type
7           , w.temperature_c_2_m_above_gnd_avg
8       from mm61_place p
9       join mm61_place_affiliation a on p.place_guid = a.parent_place_guid
10      join mm61_place c             on c.place_guid = a.place_guid
11      join mm71_weather w           on c.place_id   = w.place_id
12      where p.place_guid <> c.place_guid
13  ;
```

Sample Code 38: Place Affiliation for weather data

This simple list is for illustration purposes. The query is simplified as the mini-mart for weather has weather data at fine granularity, for example, daily entries. We can adapt the query to calculate relevant weather features like average temperature over the previous 40 days or any other aggregation that the business case requires.

| place_id | city_name | country_code | place_type | place_affiliation_type | distance_km | place_id | place_type | temperature_c_2_m_above_gnd_avg |
|----------|-----------|--------------|------------|------------------------|-------------|----------|------------|---------------------------------|
| FR00001 | a city in FR | FR | field | proximity | 15.4 | gridpoint_0048.66_0007.75 | era5 | 14.9 |
| IN.zip.591248 | Yelihadalgi | IN | zip | proximity | 6.5 | gridpoint_0016.15_0075.09 | era5 | 30.6 |
| NO.zip.6105 | Volda | NO | zip | proximity | 11.8 | gridpoint_0062.24_0006.18 | era5 | -0.1 |
| CA00003 | a city in CA | CA | field | proximity | 11.2 | gridpoint_0042.41_0081.62 | era5 | 16.6 |
| PT.zip.3840-400 | Vagos | PT | zip | proximity | 6.9 | gridpoint_0040.60_-008.63 | era5 | 15.6 |
| DE000001 | a city in DE | DE | field | proximity | 18.5 | gridpoint_0050.28_0014.51 | era5 | 13.3 |
| US000001 | a city in US | US | field | proximity | 17.0 | gridpoint_0041.98_-087.32 | era5 | 7.8 |

Figure 67: Place affiliation and weather data

## Multi-layer facts

In this example, we join facts at different granularities.

Let's quickly recap the example we already used in Figure 27 on page 55. We have committed values at the header level and planned quantities per product. They are different record_types to avoid Cartesian products-cum-inflation of committed values.

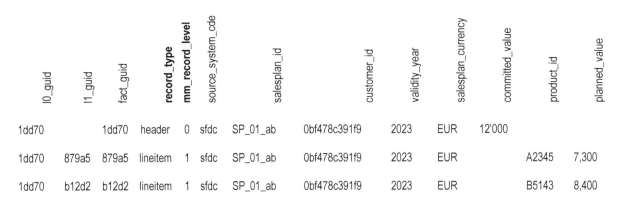

| l0_guid | l1_guid | fact_guid | record_type | mm_record_level | source_system_cde | salesplan_id | customer_id | validity_year | salesplan_currency | committed_value | product_id | planned_value |
|---------|---------|-----------|-------------|-----------------|-------------------|--------------|-------------|---------------|--------------------|-----------------|------------|---------------|
| 1dd70 | | 1dd70 | header | 0 | sfdc | SP_01_ab | 0bf478c391f9 | 2023 | EUR | 12'000 | | |
| 1dd70 | 879a5 | 879a5 | lineitem | 1 | sfdc | SP_01_ab | 0bf478c391f9 | 2023 | EUR | | A2345 | 7,300 |
| 1dd70 | b12d2 | b12d2 | lineitem | 1 | sfdc | SP_01_ab | 0bf478c391f9 | 2023 | EUR | | B5143 | 8,400 |

Figure 68: Sample data for salesplan

Querying the data is unpretentious: "return the sum of committed and planned values for year 2023."

```
1   select  validity_year
2       ,sum(committed_value)  as committed_value
3       ,sum(planned_value)    as planned_value
4       from mm05_salesplan
5       where validity_year = 2023
6       group by 1    ;
```

Sample Code 39: Simple aggregation for multi-layer facts

Multi-layer facts return the correct sum and the correct aggregation of measures regardless of their granularity. There is no risk of erroneous Cartesian sums.

The following statement is more subtle as it mentions different granularities in the same sentence. "return all planned quantities for line items for product A2345 and year 2023 where the committed value of the Salesplan is greater than 10000." It states "quantities for line items" and "committed value of the Salesplan." The sentence already hints at different granularities and this translates as such into the query.

It hints that we need a relation between measures at different granularity. They must be joined in the common column, which is l0_guid.

```
1   select  l.*
2       from mm05_salesplan l
3       join mm05_salesplan p on p.l0_guid = l.l0_guid
4                               and p.committed_value > 10000
5       where l.product_id = 'A2345'
6         and l.validity_year = 2023
7         ;
```

Sample Code 40: Self-join of multi-layer facts

Similar constructs also apply when certain data must be transposed to use as features for machine learning training.

I value the advantage of no risk of inflated totals and the simplicity of aggregations within multi-layer facts quite high, substantially higher than the complexity inherent to self-joins when requiring data at different granularity.

## Snapshot tables

Sometimes there is a business requirement for reporting values at regular intervals. One example might be reporting inventory at monthly or quarterly intervals even though inventory changes can be more frequent – or be stale. Occasionally, we meet requirements for regular reporting using snapshots of the data.

Data can become stale; inventory might not change over longer periods of time or inventory may remain 0 after a while. This begs the question of when to stop snapshotting stale data or how long to snapshot unchanged data. Should such 0 [zero] inventory be contained in any future snapshot? Do we simply not snapshot zero inventory? How about stale inventory that is not zero?

Historicization provides an elegant solution by combining a type 2 table with a master calendar,[43] Joining the master calendar and the type 2 mini-mart on calendar_date between version_from and version_to creates a limited virtual Cartesian product of entries. A query might provide the values in the mini-mart on the last day of every quarter without inflating snapshots for stale entries.

```
1    select c.calendar_date , f.*
2        from mm11_t_inventory_fact    f
3        join mm00_master_calendar     c
4            on c.calendar_date  between f.mm_version_valid_from and f.mm_version_valid_to
5            and c.calendar_date+1 = date_trunc('quarter', c.calendar_date+1)
6            and c.calendar_date <= getdate()
7        order by c.calendar_date
8    ;
```

Sample Code 41: View for a virtual snapshot table

Note the join condition on line 4 where the reported date is within the validity period of a historized version of the data and on line 5 with the condition to only select calendar dates for the last day of a quarter.

---

[43] Thank you, Chaitanya.

| calendar_date | mm_version _number | mm_version _valid_from | mm_version _valid_to | mm_version _current | Inventory _quantity |
|---|---|---|---|---|---|
| 2020-09-30 | 1 | 2020-09-09 | 2020-10-16 | false | 19'440 |
| 2020-12-31 | 3 | 2020-11-08 | 2021-04-27 | false | 0 |
| 2021-03-31 | 3 | 2020-11-08 | 2021-04-27 | false | 0 |
| 2021-06-30 | 6 | 2021-06-04 | 2021-07-01 | false | 45'360 |
| 2021-09-30 | 8 | 2021-08-06 | 2021-11-19 | false | 0 |
| 2021-12-31 | 10 | 2021-12-21 | 2022-03-25 | false | 0 |
| 2022-03-31 | 11 | 2022-03-26 | 2022-04-15 | false | 38'880 |
| 2022-06-30 | 14 | 2022-06-11 | 2022-07-06 | false | 25'920 |
| 2022-09-30 | 17 | 2022-09-16 | 2022-10-12 | false | 71'280 |
| 2022-12-31 | 19 | 2022-11-03 | 2023-01-09 | false | 0 |
| 2023-03-31 | 20 | 2023-01-10 | 2023-04-17 | false | 0 |
| 2023-06-30 | 23 | 2023-06-10 | 2023-07-05 | false | 25'920 |
| 2023-09-30 | 25 | 2023-08-16 | 2099-12-31 | TRUE | 0 |

Figure 69: Example of virtual data snapshots

It can be seen in the above table that there are consecutive quarters with no inventory change at all and quarters with multiple changes, of which only the one at the end of a quarter is reported.

This approach is free of any business assumption. It is still possible to drill down to the precise date on which a value changed; the reporting frequency can dynamically change from quarterly to monthly to weekly. If data changes more than once in a reporting period, then the query returns the values valid at the end of the reporting period. If data is stale, then stale rows are logically repeated. They are not physically repeated in the mini-mart. Therefore, there is no limit either on the granularity of the snapshot or on the duration of the snapshots. This approach provides the functionality of snapshot tables without their drawbacks.

## Machine Learning and Data Science

In this section, we focus on machine learning applications. We look at cleansing, features, and transposing a model for model training, model execution, and early assessment of a new data source's business value.

## Overview

Providing data for machine learning has facets beyond conventional BI and beyond what data pipelines for in-memory data analysis tools require.

These additional facets are summarized below and explained in the subsequent sections.

- Feature calculation

- Data cleansing and error tolerance

- Model scaling versus one-off analysis

- Persistence of data vs. persistence of pipeline

- Integrating domain-specific knowledge and/or combination with one-off data sets

- Transition from training to model execution

- Tool familiarity, such as Python data frames versus SQL/data lakehouse.

All these do not affect the design of the enterprise data lakehouse or the mini-marts as much as they affect the consumption of data and the expected data quality.

We will first look at the features and then work our way to transitioning from training to execution.

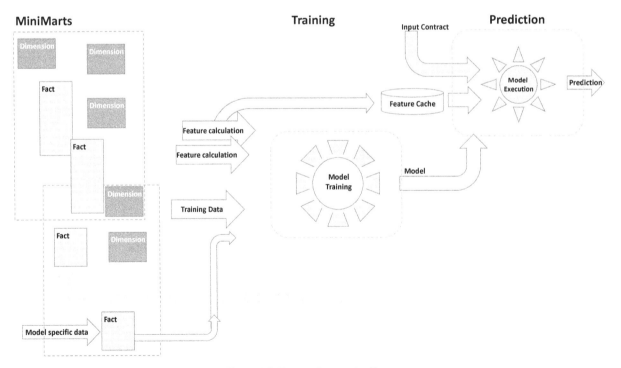

Figure 70: Data science pipeline

## Features

This section looks at feature reuse for training and execution.

Features in machine learning are individual measures or characteristics,[44] aggregated in such a way that they "best" serve the model. Examples include the longest streak of hot weather over the previous 40 days, the number of pixels in certain dimensions, or the presence, frequency, or absence of certain phrases, words, or noise ratios.

Features are often derived from data using Python code and dynamic frames. Using a modular data mart makes it possible to push feature calculations like weather patterns or spending profiles to the database backend. This has distinct advantages, not the least of which is pushing the heavy lifting to the backend database engine and reducing the amount of data transferred into the machine learning "front end." But let's first look at the difference in data requirements between model training and model execution.

Josh Wills' presentation on "building a production machine learning infrastructure"[45] at the 2014 Midwest.io was an eye-opener to me. I have not heard about his concept of the supernova since then, so I am not sure it is still used. Yet he clearly outlined the difference between model training and model execution.

While model training needs large data sets, model execution needs less data but data that is relevant for a specific execution. Let's use a specific example to explain this very generic concept. A large training set of weather conditions, soil properties, farming practices, seeds planted, and of course, trial results and observations are needed to train a model for giving advice on the best next steps. Less data is needed for executing a model. Giving advice to a farmer while driving a tractor at a specific location in her field does not require the entire range of data. It requires the relevant weather conditions and history at the farmer's current location, the type of seed she planted some weeks ago, the soil type, her farming practice, and the real-time data from the equipment sensors. What is needed is precisely the data relevant to this specific execution of a model.

No matter whether it is model training or execution, both need the same features albeit in different "dosages." Calculating features for model execution can be a time-consuming process. Pushing the feature calculation to the database backend has its advantages.

- Using the mini-mart's database engine likely enables better scaling than on an engineer's laptop and certainly less data transfer to any tool.

---

[44] https://en.wikipedia.org/wiki/Feature_(machine_learning).

[45] Josh Wills, "Building a production machine learning infrastructure," 2014 Midwest.io. https://machinelearningmastery.com/building-a-production-machine-learning-infrastructure/.

- While developing the model, the engineer can persist the data pipeline and reuse it later rather than persisting intermediate data. This makes it easier to scale a model developed for one region to other regions or, more relevantly, to re-train a model.

- When using the algorithm developed for model training later on for model execution, we can reuse the same database query, whether to calculate thousands of feature rows for training or a single specific one for this model's execution. The challenge comes with performance, whether features for model execution can and must be pre-cached. Not all columnar data stores also offer stellar performance for retrieving individual or small sets of records. Model execution, however, requires sub-second performance.

## Data quality and cleansing

This section discusses tagging erroneous data to avoid distortions of model training and execution.

Data quality is a perpetual topic. One reason is that users of the data define data quality, not the creator. Training a machine learning model can be substantially impacted by very few erroneous data points. This section outlines a subset of the data quality domain and concepts to transparently tag data quality issues and prevent them from leading to erroneous outcomes in machine learning while still allowing for model re-training.

Visual and classical BI representation of data hopefully enables the user to identify erroneous data and ignore it for decision-making, or at least there is a human filter before drawing conclusions. Training a machine learning model does not always have that luxury, especially if the model is re-trained or scaled to a wider scope or geographic area. A single outlier due to erroneous data can distort an entire model, training, and execution. Incorrect geo-coordinates are a telling example, such as latitude/longitude conflated or minus signs omitted. This results in complete distortion of models. The model training will fit its parameters embracing those erroneous data points, thereby reducing its fit for what would be correct data points. Data correction at the source and mini-mart updates are often out of reach. There may not be enough benefits to the originator of the data to invest the time or it is prevented for other reasons.

Sometimes, we can circumvent this issue by persisting intermediate data and performing multiple cleansing steps. This works well for one model but is of limited use if a model is supposed to scale or be re-trained. We saw previously that the mini-marts enable the pipeline to be persisted and not necessarily the intermediate data. This requires tagging the source data for identified data quality issues. Tagging is better than updating for transparency, so as not to lose the original values but exclude them from feature calculation.

Theoretically, we could tag on individual columns, but this might be overkill, making data usage more complex than needed. The compression of a columnar database lends itself well to row-level tagging. Tagging adds an indicator to each row, such as mm_quality_status, similar to mm_current, with values/meaning "original," "verified," "erroneous," "repaired" plus an optional qualifier column. mm_current is set to false on erroneous records with a repaired duplicate so as not to affect other data uses. Tagging records as erroneous is thus an asynchronous process we can refine continually as we learn more about actual data quality.

This way, feature calculation for both training and execution thus exclude erroneous records. Depending on requirements and impact, it only considers original or even only verified/repaired data.

## Integration of additional data

No data lakehouse will ever have all data required for a machine learning project. Additional data will almost always be needed, and a dogmatic approach to only using data from the lakehouse will fail. Additional data can simply be novel data whose business value must first be assessed. It might be data available in the enterprise or externally but not yet integrated into a mini-mart, or it might be model-specific domain data with no value outside this specific model. It can also feature parameters for classifying values or other parameters for the model. Usually, the data volume is small but its significance is high. Sometimes, rules like thresholds for value classifications are embedded into the model's code, but this is not always sufficient or prudent.

A successful data pipeline for machine learning must make it possible to combine global, integrated, and re-usable data from the marts with the long tail of "case-specific" data.

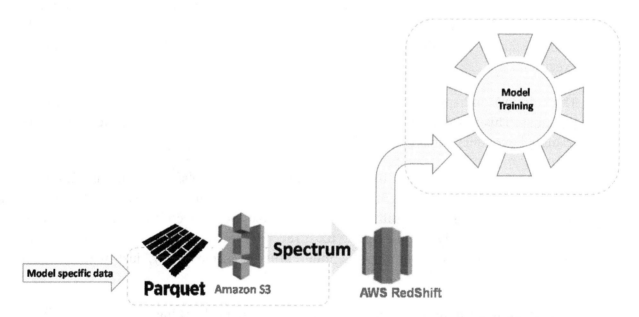

Figure 71: A technical solution for adding additional data for machine learning

Above is one of many technology examples of such an integrated approach. It uses the AWS redshift spectrum to exemplify the point, but different platforms offer different options. Additional data is often available in tabular form and can be easily converted to robust formats like parquet and then wrapped to look like a mini-mart. This approach enables complementary data to be accessed the same way as other data. It allows for creating feature queries blending specific data with global data. It provides great flexibility to data scientists. If the model proves to be of sustained value, then the complementary data can easily be converted into a mini-mart for sustained operation. Using such feature queries pushes the heavy lifting of large data volumes down to the lowest level in the technology stack, where it can be processed most effectively.

## Transition aspects

In this section, we scale and transition feature calculation from training to execution.

We discuss two noteworthy transition aspects: persistence of data versus pipeline and data manipulation.

Frequently, data used for model training is persisted in the computing platforms-cum-notebooks. This feels transparent, the data is immutable, and we can restart data manipulation for training features at any point. Creating redundant data is not really severe. This approach is well-suited for models developed and trained once. It changes if a model developed for one region proves successful and needs to be scaled wider or if it needs to be re-trained. Then all those manual steps need to be recreated.

Another alternative is no or only limited persisting of the data, and instead persist the pipeline, the SQL- and python code used to create the data set in the first place. Scaling a model's scope is then a matter of reusing those SQL queries, as is transitioning from model training to model execution.

The culmination happens if data scientists do not share data, but they share queries and data pipelines. This is a sign of a successful adoption of the approach and a means to scale model training beyond its initial scope.

The other transition aspect I have seen relates more to tools. Data scientists are often more familiar with python and dynamic frames than SQL. Therefore, feature calculation is often done in Python code. This means thinking in advance that the same code can later be used for model execution and quickly calculating the most recent feature data. Features calculated by queries make this transition easier as it is inherently the same query, just with different filter parameters.

Overall, using the mini-marts for data science and machine learning is not substantially different than any other usage, but it requires some attention to detail.

# Usage Simplification

In this section, we will help users extract values from the mini-marts even faster and adapt to changing business rules without affecting the core of the data lakehouse.

We've seen before that mini-marts are free of business interpretation. This is important in making them versatile, modular, and extensible. We can explore different business questions without knowing the precise question and granularity in advance. On the other hand, consistent business interpretation is key to the acceptance and usability of a data lakehouse. Such business interpretation is added at the consumption level, either at the level of the final query or in views on top of the mini-marts, depending on the scope and validity of the business interpretation. In either case, the rules for the business interpretation can change flexibly without affecting the underlying mini-marts. This is key to the versatility and longevity of the enterprise data lakehouse. For this, we complement the mini-marts with views.

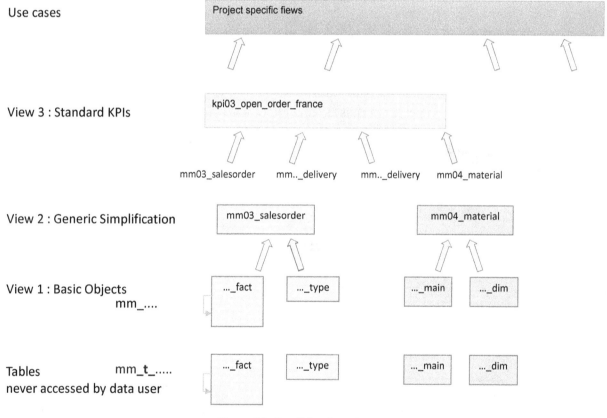

Figure 72: Simplification views

## Generic simplifications

Some views are almost always needed for basic simplifications. Examples are combining _dim with _main for dimensions, combining the description of a salesorder type with the sales order facts, or returning the most recent values only for historizing mini-marts. The example of combining the salesorder type descriptions in a view might sound puzzling, but it is much smarter to include the clear text of the description in the mini-mart right away. But descriptions can be multilingual. So we might include the preferred language description in the default view for easy use of the data while enabling the users of our mini-marts to join in with the description in any language of their choice.

We have already seen two examples of generic simplifications: the view returning only the most recent values for sales orders and the simplification view for customer data, returning exactly one entry for each unique customer_id, irrespective of how consistent or duplicative the customers are defined across the many source systems.

These simplifications are generic and are only determined by the internal design of the mini-mart, not injecting any business knowledge. They apply across the entire data lakehouse and are inherently part of any mini-mart. They are the preferred means of accessing mini-mart data unless there are very specific and well-defined requirements such as for data consistency analysis.

By convention, the default view [view mm03_salesorder_fact] returns the most recent data only, while a dedicated view [view mm03_salesorder_history] returns all data, including historical values. This is based on two assumptions: first, most usages will need actual data, and second, retaining the default name allows for seamless transition if an existing mini-mart needs to be converted to type 2. There is no change of view name for existing usages.

```
1   create view mm03_salesorder_fact as
2       select ...
3         from mm03_t_salesorder_fact
4       where mm_version_current ;
5
6   create view mm03_salesorder_history as
7       select ...
8         from mm03_t_salesorder_fact ;
```

Sample Code 42: Default views for type 2 mini-marts

## Standard KPIs

Standard KPIs build the next level of simplifications. Users hardly differentiate between pure facts or pure data and business interpretation. As diverse as it can be, business interpretation is seen as an integral part of data, and almost everyone has their own business interpretation. Nevertheless, hopefully, a few KPIs are common to some business units or countries. Those KPIs form the next level of re-usable simplification.

Some KPIs, such as the age of an order, can be determined within a mini-mart, while others can be a combination of multiple mini-marts. We have seen examples of the latter on order quantities not yet delivered, a combination of sales order and aggregated delivery data. Additionally, KPIs can contain specific business rules like "business day 5" being the day for a period shift. The definition of the previous month and current month "moves one month forward" on business day 5. We can code such definitions into standard KPI views.

These standard KPIs views can be global but apply to specific regions or business units with their own, unique definition of KPIs. That validity defines the scope and naming convention for such views. The business rules for such KPIs can change, which is reflected in the views. The mini-marts themselves do not change since they capture business facts without interpretation. Such KPI views need strong governance and a dedicated business owner. Automated data lineage will help the governance and transparency of such views.

## Project-specific views

Combining mini-marts into entire business questions must be flexible and agile and quickly adapt to changing requirements or iterations of the original business question. Generally, solutions can be implemented faster if fewer people need to be involved and fewer components are changed. Embedding project-specific queries directly inside the analysis or reporting application is the most agile approach. In this sense, there should be no reason for "use case-specific view" as each use case is unique. Otherwise, it would be a standard KPI. Despite this attractive theory, practice has shown that users prefer "ready-made" data for their use case, as unique as it is. This is made easier with use case- or project-specific views. Their ownership must be as close to the "consuming user" as possible, ideally a data analyst in a business function.

There is another valid reason for use-case-specific views. The transition of machine learning from training to operation and the scaling of machine learning are made easier if we calculate features at the backend and these calculations coined into views and reused across applications.

# NINE

# Data Catalog and Lineage

This chapter outlines how to empower users to find and trust the data in the enterprise data lakehouse. A trusted data catalog is vital for data as a product. The solutions to data catalog and lineage presented herein come from experience. They are only one of many possible approaches and are not meant as the ultimate solution. However, a data catalog has three primary functions: make data findable, explain data usage, and define the naming conventions for the common dimensions.

## Data catalog

In theory, data is self-explanatory. The naming convention on the columns ought to give a precise description. In practice, we need additional information to make data truly understandable.

The data catalog should contain descriptions for every column and table, plus an overview of the mini-mart. This overview for each mini-mart could contain:

| | |
|---|---|
| Summary | A brief business purpose and overview of this mini-mart's content. Sometime it is helpful to add a disambiguation in here, not unlike the ones in Wikipedia. |
| Source system and scope | Different source systems add different data to the mini-mart. This part lists the scope and time horizon for each contributing source system. Scope can be geographic or organizational; time horizon is relevant for historical data, for example, all sales data since 2010. |
| Summary of views/access points | A summary of the APIs and the views for retrieving the mini-mart's content. The details of each API and view are then best described on respective detail "pages." |

| | |
|---|---|
| Identifiers | Columns in business terms to uniquely identify each record. The different types of identifiers are described individually. |
| Business Keys | The business identifiers relevant to retrieving the data. |
| | These are not the technical identifiers like fact_guid but the identifiers for accessing the data in business terms, the _dims and the respective counterparts in _facts. |
| | If applicable, this section lists and describes the different identifier types for the synonyms of dimensions and source system. |
| Classifying columns | The classifying columns supplement the business keys, also known as dimensions. They are essential to differentiate generalized entries. |
| | These can be *record_types*, *cost-types*, *product-categories*, explicit source systems, or any other columns needed to classify a record but too "small" to justify becoming a full-fledged dimension. |
| Common dimensions | All references to dimensions. |
| | This list can be derived automatically via naming conventions; adding it explicitly helps with understanding. |
| Multi-layer facts | Where applicable. Describing the logical data model within the mini-mart, the various record-types, and the relations between them. |
| Sample queries | Sample queries using this mini-mart, either/or in context with other data or in filtered and aggregated form. |
| Detailed description | The business context of the data in the mini-mart. This gives the reason behind the content and design of the mini-mart. |
| | Some mini-marts might have a small ER model embedded within them, such as the ones that contain multi-lingual codes or dependent objects. The mini-mart's ER model should be shown and explained in this section. |
| Data Quality and Data Consistency | In theory, this section should not exist or should just state whether there are any data quality issues. In reality, mini-marts can have known data deficiencies. These can be missing data at the source or data quality issues, such as the source system not validating certain information. Listing these known issues promotes trust in the data in the mini-mart and, at best, creates awareness of data issues with the data originator. |
| Update frequency | Update frequency and timing per source system, whether continuous streaming data in 30-second batches, every hour or once a day at 5:00 a.m. UST |
| Contacts | It helps to know a knowledgeable person behind every mini-mart, potentially per source system. Ideally, this is a data steward for business content plus a technical contact. |
| Release Notes | Which sources have been added when and other changes to the mini-mart. |

It is hardly possible to automatically generate meaningful descriptions of data objects beyond the trivial ones. Nevertheless, automatically including all existing objects, tables, and columns in the catalog enables identifying objects needing further content descriptions. We can create similar documentation for the standard KPI views.

In addition, automated data cataloging helps with data mesh. It allows fragmented marts to be cataloged and column alignment and granularity to be compared. This facilitates virtual generalized marts across multiple nodes. This provided data catalog is more than just a hierarchical thesaurus. It must visualize the connections and reuse between objects as an intuitive network.

Data engineers might tend to focus on the technical delivery of mini-marts or focus on the next project. They might treat documenting mini-marts as a second priority. This "habit" undermines the trust in and uptake of the enterprise lakehouse. Having complete and user-focused documentation has become one of the greatest and most persistent challenges. People tend to invent parallel solutions if data is not understood and understandable. The tendency to treat documentation as a second priority can be partially controlled by rating the completeness of the mini-mart's documentation, embedding documentation in go-live checklists, and inviting users to contribute to a mini-mart's documentation. But most importantly, the mindset must be on "[document] data as a [marketable] product."

## Common dimensions

The data catalog is also the point of reference for common dimensions. Their documentation could contain:

| Documentation Heading | Content |
| --- | --- |
| Name | The column name of the common dimension such as *customer_idd*. These names must be used in fact_table to refer to them; if needed prefixed with qualifiers like *sold_to_*customer_idd. |
| Description | A brief description of this common dimension. This is a good place to remind users of the generalizations behind this dimension. |
| Identifier examples | Some examples of the identifiers for illustration. |
| Data transformation | The rules for the identifiers. Sample instructions, such as: without leading zeros, all lowercase, and no space. This is also the place where the rules for disambiguation and qualifiers are defined for entries like sapab.6125345 or salesoffice.34. |

## Lineage

The mini-marts in our data lakehouse integrate data from multiple source systems. We can use them without intrinsic knowledge of source systems. Yet people naturally think in "source systems" when they describe a topic. They just do not want the hassle of it. As the uptake of the enterprise lakehouse increases, users will start asking questions about the origin and content of the mini-marts. They want to know the source systems tables and columns feeding a certain column in a mini-mart. They'll also ask whether a certain source systems table and column is included in the lakehouse, in which mini-mart and column. Getting answers to these questions enhances trust in the lakehouse. In addition, data engineers and project managers want to do impact analysis and know which mini-mart is used by whom and how, directly or through views, and which mini-marts are rarely used. This is where lineage comes into play. Lineage complements the metadata in the data catalog. It enables forward and backward searches of data origin, availability in mini-marts, and ultimately end-usage. Yet there are two challenges: getting lineage data in the first place and translating it into actionable insights. We can address the former with flow analysis tools such as SQLflow.[46] Those tools can automate lineage analysis, keeping the information always up-to-date. Yet lineage tends to result in complex graphs of data flows. Figure 73 shows the incoming and outgoing flow on the example of material master data. This mini-mart consolidates data from eleven source systems into a seemingly simple object like material master data. Each edge or connection between nodes corresponds to an SQL statement in our ETL processes.

Figure 73: Detailed lineage data too complex for insights

These graphs are overwhelming and too detailed for insights. They must be condensed. The most compressed forms are simple lists and graphs showing the original data source/table/columns related to the destination column in the mini-mart without all the clutter in between. These graphs and lists essentially compress the graph between the leftmost point, which is a source system and table, and the mini-marts table and column. This simple form is understandable and helpful to data scientists, data users, and visualization engineers. They enable seeing the wood for the tree, facilitate adoption, and reduce the likelihood of creating duplicate mini-marts. Linking from there into the graph allows drilling down to the individual steps if needed.

---

[46] SQLflow from https://www.gudusoft.com/.

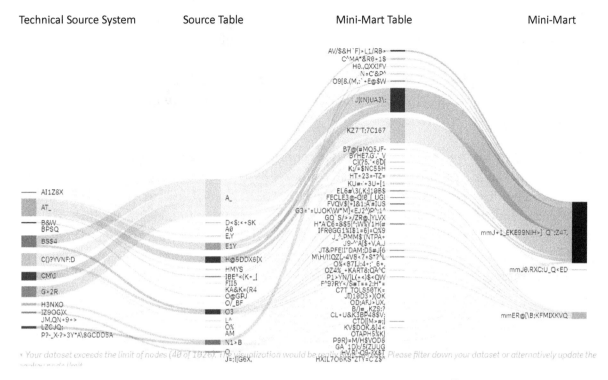

Figure 74: Lineage flow at source and target table level[47]

The almost finest level of lineage information provides insights for individual columns, listing the detailed source columns for every column in the mini-mart.

|  | | ECC1 | ECC2 | sfdc |
|---|---|---|---|---|
| 04: Product Info - Material | | - | - | - |
| | volume | marm.volume; | marm.volume; | - |
| | volume_uom | marm.volume_unit; | marm.volume_unit; | - |
| | abc_indicator | marc.abc_indicator; | marc.abc_indicator; | - |
| | apportionment_structure | mkal.csplt; | - | - |
| | special_procurement_type | marc.special_procurement_type; mkal.sobsl; | marc.special_procurement_type; | - |
| mm14 SalesTerritory | | | | |
| | sales_office_idd | knvv.vkbur; | - | - |
| | sales_org_cde | knvv.vkorg; | - | - |
| | sales_territory_description | knvv.bzirk; knvv.spart; knvv.vkbur; knvv.vkgrp; knvv.vkorg; knvv.vtweg; | - | territory2.description; |

Figure 75: Lineage reporting at column level

---

[47] The sample data is obfuscated on purpose.

In addition to upstream lineage, downstream lineage supports priority-setting and impact analysis, regardless of whether a mini-mart is used directly or through a view. Downstream lineage should extend all the way to the query statement, the user who executed it, and the interaction frequency. We can identify unused objects and resources focused on where they return the most value. Upstream and downstream lineage are twins and can be addressed with the same toolset.

Some organizations might have multiple reports and visualizations with similar content. This is simply because it is difficult to classify reports by their business content and identify existing reports with similar content before creating new ones. Downstream lineage helps classify reports. Lineage allows the identifying of all reports containing, for example, inventory and process order together with sales forecast. This is because the description of mini-marts is in business terms and lineage links those mini-marts to actual usages. Together they provide a concise and automated classification of reports and visualizations.

# TEN

# Transition Challenges

This last chapter focuses on adapting mindsets and unlearning legacy techniques. The transition challenge might be a very individual one. The particular outline provided here is based on a large legacy organization with substantial outsourcing to contractors, a legacy data warehouse, and the conventional tendency to siloed data. The transition challenge focuses on data as a product, knowledge and teams, and ownership. It is an incomplete list and does not apply in all circumstances. Read it with a healthy dose of caution, as food for thought, in keeping with the maxim "better safe than sorry."

The biggest challenge, however, is imagination, liberating thinking from former constraints such as data silos and hard walls between systems. The total is bigger than the sum of its parts. An organization must overcome those mental blockers, otherwise, they remain stuck in how it was always done.

## Data as a Product

Times have changed and data access is more commonly granted to consumers outside the data creator function. Nevertheless, it is a mindset change to genuinely embrace sharing and documenting data across an organization so others can benefit. Surprisingly, the bigger, more tangible change sometimes is focusing on business meaning rather than technology. Users and data engineers alike tend to think in terms of source systems. I have seen mini-marts that are essentially copies of the source system tables. While knowledge of the source system is important for translating its data into business meaning, the data in the mini-mart reflects the business meaning. One should not need to know how the various source system's tables connect. That's one reason why data is denormalized. Just think of the phrase, "This record tells me that…." There is no techno-lingo in that sentence.

A mini-mart obviously reconciles with the individual source system tables' content, but more importantly, it matches with the user's screen and UI for interacting with the data. That leap in mindset from a technical implementation viewpoint to a business-meaning viewpoint can be more challenging than expected. Always request a copy of a user's screen before designing any mini-mart to understand how a user sees the information and verify clarity about the phrase I have repeated several times: "This record tells me that..."

Shared data usage, making data available as a product, requires documenting the data in a way that consumers can comprehend and use outside the data originator function. "Data as a Product." It sounds trivial, yet documenting a mini-mart, its tables, views, and columns in business terms is not a favorite pastime of data engineers. In other words, it is a cultural shift making business user documentation an integral part of any delivery and doing this no matter the pressure from new demands. Implementing and sustaining rigorous documentation quality standards is probably one of the biggest cultural shifts. Many other aspects then derive from it.

## Knowledge and technology

This section looks at the capabilities and knowledge of data engineers and data architects. Obviously, they must have a sound understanding of SQL or the transformation technology chosen. Yet having extensive experience in the database technology chosen for the mini-mart is good but not crucial to success. The various technologies are similar enough that having a select few individuals with profound understanding of the technology is sufficient. It is far more important for data engineers and architects to have a sound understanding of data and data models, be able to see connections, and ask questions until they capture the true, clear business meaning. They must be able to "put themselves in the shoes of a business user" while remaining conceptually consistent.

This kind of knowledge manifests itself in a few areas, especially generalization. Distilling the true business meaning makes it possible to identify the superclass for an object, irrespective of its source systems. Inventory at a distributor is still inventory, albeit channel inventory, no matter whether a distributor in Japan uses different systems than retailers in the US and whether we get the same level of detail from both. Recognizing those classes, those generalizations, requires a shift in focus from systems to data, yet once this takes place, it proves to be immensely powerful and cost-effective.

As stated earlier, the ETL processes must be robust. No data must be lost, data supplied twice must not result in duplicate data in the mini-marts. A robust process must not depend on the source systems' awareness of data already sent. Again, this sounds trivial, yet embracing that level of resilience might call for a change of mindset.

Lastly, a word about data types, which may seem trivial but is not always obvious. Many source systems, especially older ones, are constrained in their data types. They have, in essence, numbers and characters. These systems store dates as character strings [20231212]. In the mini-mart these are of datatype date or datetime, not a string. Likewise, Booleans are not "1,""0," "X" or "yes" like they are in many source systems, but datatype Booleans. Similarly, blanks in descriptions and other string fields are true <null>, not empty strings. It can be surprisingly difficult for people used to more conventional systems to abstract data types. Making this leap is part of the shift from a focus on technology to a focus on data meaning. It is a pre-requisite that data can be used irrespective of and across source systems.

## Data engineering / delivery teams

We have seen that there are essentially three steps in the ETL process besides designing the mini-marts: physically acquiring the data from the source into the staging area, transforming the data and loading it into the mini-marts, and lastly, data usage for feeding machine learning or the various maturity levels of data reporting and analytics.

The first step, data acquisition, requires technical knowledge of source systems and experience with technology but only limited business and data engineering capabilities. A dedicated team focusing on mastering the diverse source system technologies might address this step best.

Transforming the data into modular, integrated marts requires a solid grasp of data models and data engineering. It requires knowledge of generic business processes and the data's meaning. It always goes back to that basic phrase: "This row tells me that...." It requires interpreting the data and translating it into business meaning. This step is best assigned to business analysts/data engineers/data architects with some conceptual understanding of the business processes. They can translate the data into the simplest form while preserving all information.

Data usage requires no knowledge of source system technology and limited data engineering knowledge. Still, it does require sound business expertise and sound knowledge of how business questions translate into data questions. This is equally valid for data visualization and data science; both need domain knowledge. It might help to structure the data delivery along the following lines: a data acquisition team centering around the source system technology and staging area; focused roles for business analysts, data architects, and data engineers for transforming the raw data into the integrated, simplified mini-marts; and business teams focusing on data re-usage/visualization/data science, analytics, and data usage in any shape and form. These teams could include business analysts, translating the original question, the "Ask," into the nouns and data needed and then into analysis, closing the circle.

## Ownership

Data in an integrated data lakehouse must have descriptions and data owners. Originally, I grossly underestimated the latter, naïvely assuming that it was sufficient if the content in the mini-marts matched the data in the source systems in a coherent, integrated, and accessible way. I was mistaken. Any mini-mart must have a business owner who confirms correctness and acts as a trustee. That role is sourced from the business function that owns or creates the data and is established in the first project that needs the respective data. The business owner also reviews the mini-mart's documentation and plays a continuous role in approving access to the mart.

We have seen that the first project needing specific data triggers getting that data into a mini-mart in the first place. Let's assume the original request was for production and supply. At that time, the mini-mart will likely be owned and delivered by a team focusing on production and supply. Yet any mini-mart can be cross-functional or used for different purposes. For example, for production and supply, commercial analysis, or a wider range of countries. Over time, the same mini-mart might contain data from additional sources.

While individual flows/source systems feeding one and the same mini-mart are largely independent of each other, there is nevertheless an implied ownership or accountability for the entire mini-mart. One could say that each of those teams could create its own mesh node. While this is correct, I would caution from creating a too fine-grain data mesh where the same business objects consolidate data from different domains. I don't think it is optimal if each domain creates its own node for common business objects like materials, locations, or basic customer data. In such cases, it is beneficial if multiple teams jointly contribute to the same object. It sounds trivial, but human behavior sometimes gets in the way. It requires a mindset change empowering cross-team contributions. For example empowering the team supporting commercial analysis to add data to a mini-mart originally developed by production and supply. Such collaboration is vital and made easier as multiple workflows into the same mini-mart are independent from each other.

---

## Things that should have been done better

I conclude with a short summary of experiences from an actual implementation, looking at what could have been done better or different with the 20/20 benefit of hindsight. The list below is neither complete nor representative but makes a fitting conclusion.

- **Architectural rigor.** No mini-mart development should start before the data engineer has a screen/UI showing how the user sees the data and before she has created and reviewed a simple example-mini-mart Excel sheet. The latter is part of the specification; it reveals misunderstandings and confirms common understandings, such as disambiguated business keys, while the former is very useful as an early unit test.

- **Business ownership.** Establish business ownership for data from the very beginning.

- **Common objects** Organizations might have sets of terms and objects that are widely used. Such data, such as lists of countries, organizations, currencies, and sites, is often trivial. They are so "common" they might not have a formal owner. They also do not have a champion. These mini-marts should be developed with rigor very early in the process.

- **KPI views.** Countries and business units define KPIs in a large variety of ways. Having the pure facts in the mini-marts is essential but not sufficient. Set focus earlier on creating country and business unit-specific KPI views.

- **Elementary mini-marts.** Some of our first mini-marts were sourced from cubes from a legacy data warehouse. Those cubes, in turn, were an amalgam of different objects in the same source system, such as sales orders, deliveries, and invoices. In hindsight, we should have created the individual elementary mini-marts and the KPI view right from the outset, even if it meant reverse engineering the logic of the legacy warehouse whose documentation had long been lost and forgotten.

- **Documentation.** Haste is not a valid reason to shortcut documentation. No mini-mart should ever be released into the wild before the business owner confirms that its documentation is correct and complete. Documentation is essential as it allows existing data to be reused instead of creating new copies and saves money in the long term.

- **Data quality and monitoring.** Users will always find that one mismatched record among millions. Data quality, correctness, and completeness are crucial to acceptance. Reasoned consistency checks must be incorporated into the delivery and routine operation processes.

- **Delivery speed.** New mini-marts can be implemented very fast, sometimes in hours or, at most, days. A small team of business-savvy data engineers can quickly cycle between business understanding and formal mini-mart design. Preserve that focus on quick delivery even as teams grow bigger and processes demand more formalization.

- **Wrappers and technology.** ETL processes, while ultimately coded in SQL, are to a great extent standardized and repeatable, especially the upsert also known as load steps. The wrapper for these SQLs can be standardized early on. It helps ease mundane coding chores like coding synchronous lists of columns and allows for efficient deployment mechanisms.

- **Security**. The mini-marts were originally intended to be used only by front-end tools with embedded security and access restriction mechanisms. Anticipate that actual use will be much broader and more generic, so plan a dedicated security layer at the earliest.

- **The SQL gap.** The original users, such as data scientists and visualization engineers, are mostly familiar with SQL. The lack of a no-coding tool for retrieving data from the mini-marts was not a big issue for them. Yet, as self-service interest grew in the business user community, the lack of such a no-coding-SQL tool was a hindrance. Bridging the SQL gap should have been addressed earlier.

# Summary

This book described techniques and methodology for modular data marts. They are suitable for mature enterprises resulting from various merges and acquisitions and having a heterogeneous system landscape.

A business question is often a series of facts and rules strung together in specific ways. These "data journeys" address specific questions, combining information in relation to each other. To illustrate the above, we used the analogy of a toy railway. Answering specific questions means stringing the individual track pieces or mini-marts together and "traveling" from one object or "piece of knowledge" to the next.

Our approach scales linearly, not exponentially, as the data lakehouse's scope increases. I realized later that this makes it well-suited for designing a data mesh. It enables autonomy for individual mesh nodes. Each mesh node can evolve individually. They all contribute to a consistent, integrated environment where the total is bigger than the sum of its parts. The data marts can grow with the business, adapt to changing and evolving needs, and integrate data irrespective of source system, technology, or function.

The model proposed in this book is a hybrid model, a snowflake model on steroids. The Model is ETL to the point of conformed and modular mini-marts, yet those mini-marts do not predefine the schema for querying nor constrain the business questions.

Mini-marts can be distributed across the various nodes of a data mesh. This is because they are independent of each other, can even have independent workflows into the same consolidated mart, and inherently use synonyms to cope with different identifiers for the same "thing" across the enterprise. They are source system agnostic, at the finest grain, generalized and implicit assumptions are made explicit. They use conformed natural business keys as common dimensions to connect with each other. Those keys can be disambiguated where needed.

The mini-marts are highly generalized, making it more transparent for users to filter for a data subset in a mini-mart than it is to search for a different mart with similar data. Each mini-mart contains a small set of physical tables, in many cases, just one. The entire enterprise data lakehouse is built using only two different design blueprints: facts and dimensions.

A key phrase when designing a mini-mart is:

"This record tells me that ........"

Our model captures the "facts" about any object without interpretation. However beware of Cartesian products or measures at mixed granularities. They can result from JSON arrays or other constellations where data might be joined incorrectly. Multi-layer facts are an elegant way to circumvent those risks. They are strictly for situations where the finest grain sources inherently have measures at different granularity within the same business object. Querying those facts does not require special business knowledge.

Internal technical keys of transactional systems should never be exposed and used outside the original transactional system. Our data lakehouse must solely rely on data that is exposed by the source system for external usage. Using business keys is more transparent and understandable for the user.

The mini-marts consolidate data from various systems and are based on natural business keys, namely the _IDs in the _dim tables. When combined, there is no guarantee that the same value for one key [_id] means the same everywhere. This is where disambiguation and qualifying are needed. While data consolidation comes easy for fact data, consolidation is a bit trickier for dimensions. There are two fundamentally different approaches to this consolidation: hard and soft consolidation. The choice between them is business-driven. In short, use hard consolidation if you are certain that the entry with the same key really means the same "thing" in all systems and use soft consolidation if this is not so sure.

Our model organization can have many terms for one "thing." Consequently, the model anticipates that every object has synonyms and flexible hierarchies. The former results in the dimension's _dim table, the latter in the _affiliation and _ladder tables.

Hierarchies are ubiquitous in any enterprise. Sometimes they are balanced and have the same number of levels in all sub-trees, and sometimes they are not. Affiliations and ladder reflect relationships and hierarchies within the same mini-mart. The different viewpoints are captured in the dedicated column *affiliation_type*.

There are different techniques for physically integrating data: data virtualization versus integration, such as co-located marts or data lakehouses. The data model concepts proposed in this book can work with both techniques.

ETL (Extract, Transform, and Load,) and ELT (Extract, Load, and Transform) can be done regularly, for example, hourly, daily, or continuously. It must be robust and prevent duplications, preferably load delta data only, transparent, and self-correcting in case something goes missing.

Transform is the core of the data pipeline. It captures the "business knowledge." The transform step condenses the application-specific tables of the source system into business meaning for easy understanding and use. The steps after transform are highly generic and can be industrialized. There are just three variations: "normal basic load" preventing duplications, historicization (type 2) if data changes need to be tracked, and special precautions for atomic lists.

Any enterprise data warehouse or lakehouse is never complete. Additional columns might be needed, the mini-mart might need historicization, additional sources may be added contributing to the same mini-mart. Mini-marts can be extended easily provided implicit assumptions about data are made explicit and there are no physical limits.

Sometimes there is a business requirement for reporting values at regular intervals. One example might be reporting inventory at monthly or quarterly intervals, even though inventory changes can be more frequent or stale. Occasionally, requirements for regular reporting are met using snapshots of the data. Yet data can become stale. Historicization provides an elegant solution by combining a type 2 table with a master calendar.

Providing data for machine learning has facets beyond conventional BI and beyond what data pipelines for in-memory data analysis tools require. Focus on feature calculation, data cleansing, and model scaling. The modular data pipeline allows persisting the pipeline, not the data itself, making afore mentioned steps easier to repeat.

Mini-marts are free of business interpretation. This is an important factor in making them so versatile, modular, and extensible. On the other hand, users hardly differentiate between pure facts or pure data and business interpretation. Consistent business interpretation on top of the pure facts is key to the acceptance and usability of a data lakehouse. Such business interpretation is added at the consumption level, either at the level of the final query or in views on top of the mini-marts. In either case, the rules for the business interpretation can change flexibly without affecting the underlying mini-marts.

A trusted data catalog is vital for a data lakehouse. It is pivotal for data as a product. In theory, data is self-explanatory. The naming convention on the columns ought to give a precise description. In practice, additional information is needed to make data truly understandable. A data catalog must be semi-automatic. It must parse the data lakehouse and automatically capture all existing objects, tables, and columns. This guarantees at least completeness of the metadata and allows "filling in the blanks" with specific content. Data engineers might tend to focus on delivery mini-marts or focus on the next project and treat documenting them as a second priority. This "habit" undermines the trust in and uptake of mini-marts.

The mini-marts in our data lakehouse integrate data from multiple source systems. Data scientists and visualization engineers use and combine the data with no intrinsic knowledge of any source system. But people naturally think in "source systems," they just don't want to be bothered. Despite this, knowing precisely where data originates is crucial in adopting any consolidated data marts.

The lineage challenge is twofold. The first is getting end-to-end lineage information from complex multi-technology environments and the second is condensing it to actionable insights. The entire lineage documentation process should be fully automated, hence always up-to-date. Dedicated tools like SQLflow help this process.

The transition must cope with cultural aspects, knowledge and technology, team organization, and data ownership.

The biggest challenge, however, is imagination, liberating our thinking from former constraints, data silos, and hard walls. A whole new world in data insights opens once we overcome these barriers.

# Index

www.ingramcontent.com/pod-product-compliance
Lightning Source LLC
Chambersburg PA
CBHW080532060326
40690CB00022B/5106